The GIFT
of CANCER

A Call to Awakening

ANNE McNERNEY

Edited by Gemma Bridges.
Design by Kathleen Ryan.

First printing
10 9 8 7 6 5 4 3 2 1

ISBN: 0-9668716-5-0

resonant publishing

Baltimore, Maryland
www.resonantgroup.com

With L O V E:

To my favorite contrarian, Frank,
and my wonderful kids,
Kaitlyn, Kelsey, Bree, Frankie, and Lindsey.

I refuse to settle for something less,
Or second best, like all the rest.
I denounce the packaged, planned neat little life
Where I am not a woman, but merely a wife.
They do what is best for me
In their own eyes.
But who will <u>see</u> for me after they die?
Please let me start now and make my mistakes
And if I never <u>wake up</u> it won't be too late...

F A L L, *1976*

FOREWORD

I don't know where to start. I keep waiting for something to start for me. After a year now, I realize that nothing is going to happen until I do something. I have felt for some time that I have something to say. I have tried to say it to a select few, to close friends, family, people I feel comfortable with. But to no avail. My message continues to fall on deaf ears. Or people really don't have an interest. In any event, it is just not working like I expected. Actually that's not true; I've had many expectations, none of which have materialized.

My husband Frank asked, "Just how many books are you going to read, how many experts are you going to pursue? Where do you think you are going to get the 'green light' to move forward with what you want to say?" And he's right of course. I have been waiting for someone to lift me into this area of expertise.

I have been waiting for others to discover me. I have been passively looking for a guru to recognize the guru within me. I have spent the first half of my life believing that doing a good job, exceeding others expectations of what they wanted of me would bring recognition, reward and ultimately happiness. I suppose this is one of life's lessons. To initiate, to risk failure, to begin the second half of my life leading my life, not waiting for someone else to authenticate my life.

And so this book. Because nothing else seems to make more sense.

My message is simply this. The time has come to seriously examine the connection between spirituality and illness. In particular, cancer. You see, I can write about this because 10 years ago I had cancer. And, as part and parcel of that experience, cancer triggered my awakening. The motivation for this book is to pull on the strings that bind the mystery of cancer. Not the biology of cancer, not the molecular structure of cancer, but the origin of cancer – the *need* for cancer. I am afraid and excited at the same time.

I must tell you that exploring the connection between illness and spirit has become a very emotional issue for me. I can state unequivocally that this is now my passion. I have never had a passion before. A passionate person, without a passion. Does that make sense? There are people who wake up every day revved with a passion for sports car racing, cooking, cleaning, mountain climbing, drawing, painting, building, dancing. And then there was me. Passionate in nature about basically nothing. Nothing, of course, until I got cancer.

And, honestly, for several years afterward, I did my best to suppress my growing curiosity with the spiritual, sometimes mystical, aspects of this disease. I thought that what happened to me was only for me; it was my personal experience. I didn't trust my own instincts to think outside the box about something like cancer. I left that to the experts. Like millions of others, I was treated with conventional medicine, fared pretty well and returned to my life. Returned to my routine, as best I could. Actually, I wandered from one day to the next doing what I was "supposed" to do.

Prior to getting cancer, I never thought about it, never feared getting it, never was sick a day in my life, other than a case of the flu or normal childhood illnesses every so often. I rarely got colds, was healthy as a horse; had a beyond-boring medical file. Like you, probably, I resented paying health insurance.

Do you recognize yourself here? Do I sound like you, like every man? Then trust in what I am about to tell you. Trust that if you are experiencing cancer, or know someone who is, that my experience can be your experience. Stay open and stay with me.

First of all, let me say there is a *knowing* of cancer. A knowing before the doctors know. Then there is tremendous fear, the fear of not being in control. The anxiety is unbearable. Then there is the reality of what the doctors tell you. But that is their reality; it doesn't have to be yours or your loved ones'. Those are their experiences, their statistics, their medicine. But they don't know you. They don't know what makes you tick, what keeps you going. And maybe you don't even know. But cancer will certainly help you find out. Cancer will lead you to God. Let me say that again. Cancer is your connection to the Divine.

I am talking about the spirituality of illness. The place hope takes you, where medicine can't. If you think of medicine as the mechanical device used to fix the broken parts of your machine, your body, then consider Spirit (or lack thereof) as that part of you that determines whether you stay healthy or become ill, that part of you of which you may be, at this juncture, totally unaware.

I will tell you my story from beginning until end. I will tell you how I became aware of my own sense of spirit through my dreams and how these dreams played a tremendous role in my conscious life. You will see in the pages ahead that I don't always understand the dream, but that there is a definite connection, a communication that I have only now come to realize will be my life's work. My passion, if you will.

"...it is important that we tell each other our experiences in Spirit. At any point someone could make a leap because you are living and speaking a truth that person is ready to grasp."

GLORIA D. KARPINSKY

Where Two Worlds Meet

THE BEGINNING

Picture a woman in her late 30s, navy suit, navy pumps, throwing kids in the car, always behind the eight ball, always rushing madly. Preschool 8:05, school 8:15; work 8:30. Traffic lights, forgotten homework, nothing taken out for dinner, laundry taking on a life of its own, the faint smell of Gerber's somewhere close to her nostrils. It could be the jacket, the scarf, worse yet the blouse. Anyway, you get the picture. Saturdays, I'm up at dawn to defeat the laundry, Sunday groceries, etc. Maybe if I'm really lucky I might catch 60 minutes to watch *60 Minutes*. Of course the race begins again Monday. There is no quality time for husband, children, friends, you, and quite frankly, why indulge yourself when you're back to the grind before you know it.

Furthermore, I was unaware. This is a very important point. I was unaware. What was I doing? What was I proving and to whom? I had to prove to *myself* that I could balance fourteen balls at one time. I had to have every situation under control. It was part of my basic nature. I felt I would be judged by how well I handled the curve balls life threw my way. And yet really, who cared? Would it be written on my tombstone: "here lies a woman who ran herself ragged?" Wow!

The point of the matter is I had bought the whole feminist movement – hook, line and sinker. I wanted it all. I wanted a great career, great marriage and great kids. I wanted all of this at whatever cost. I guess you could say I was a raving overachiever. In the midst of this frenzy, this frenetic activity, there was no time to reflect on anything other than if the laundry was caught up. And I believe it was at this time that my body grew cancer.

While I suspect when it started, there is no way to know definitely. But that's not the point. The point is that cancer hit me upside the head! It brought all the craziness to a screeching halt. Within a matter of days, all the air was out of my sails, I was set to sea adrift with no wind, no course to follow, just days of dark blue, frightening sea.

✦ ✦ ✦

It's one of those Saturdays. I'm almost on top of my game; it's early afternoon, and for some reason, everyone is taking a nap! Surely a miracle in itself. And so rather than do what I would normally do, which is laundry (always laundry), I stole a nap in my son's room. When I woke up, I reached under my arm because I thought there was a sock or something lodged in the sleeve of my sweater. Actually, that's not exactly right. Let me rephrase that. When I awoke, there was a suggestion *sitting* on my mind to look for something lodged in my armpit. And so, with that thought, I reached deep under my arm and discovered not a sock but a lump the size of a peach seed. Not thinking a whole lot about it, other than it was odd and in an odd place, I resumed my Saturday insanity with my normal vigor.

Weeks passed before I finally had it checked out. And while my internist didn't dismiss it, he certainly didn't give me any cause for alarm.

After examining me, he suggested I stop down the hall and get an x-ray. So while sitting in the waiting room, I spotted an article in Newsweek or some such magazine on cancer. And before I can complete the insurance forms, my eyes well uncontrollably. My body was reacting to the word "cancer." There in that small, pleasant office, amidst a half dozen total strangers, my gut was telling me I had cancer, a condition I had never thought about. My body was acting totally out of my control, totally independent from me. Nothing could have prepared me for that moment. It was all very surreal. The pen in my hand was completing the forms, but I wasn't there. I was somewhere closeby watching this odd little display of emotions. What a strange sensation: to feel warm tears streaming down my face and yet not connect it with any feeling other than maybe mild surprise.

It was a 20 minute walk home from the doctor's. As if lifted from my physical form, I watched myself go through the rest of the motions that afternoon. It was late spring; the azaleas were full with color. As I walked I took in everything around me. Each step was more pronounced than the last. Somehow I knew that soon I would walk a different path and that my life would never be the same. I would never live in that moment again.

By the time I made it home, there was no convincing me otherwise – I had cancer. Despite the fact that the blood work and x-rays were normal; the fact that there was no history in my family, that everyone, (including my rational side), thought I was overreacting, and the fact that no doctor had given me the slightest hint that it could be cancer, I *knew* I had it. And so weeks later when it was finally confirmed by the surgeon, I was relieved. Yes, relieved to finally know that I know what I know. To receive outside validation of what some part of me inside knew all along.

As it turned out, the official report from my surgeon was that I had a rare form of breast cancer. A type that appears in the lymph nodes adjacent to the breast tissue, but not in the breast itself. Again, I am relieved to find out that I have a common form of cancer, one I at least recognize by name.

I knew women who had survived breast cancer, old women, and young women. This was good news. Again, this is a situation I could handle. As I look back, if it had been named anything else I think I would have reacted very badly. But hearing that it was breast cancer was palatable. Because, remember, the real shock of having cancer had hit me weeks before, weeks before anyone else knew.

We left the surgeon's and before going home, Frank, who was pretty shook up, suggested we stop by St. Mary's, our parish church, to collect our thoughts. From the bright mid-day sun of that hot, humid Baltimore day, we silently ushered into the cool darkness of St. Mary's, and slipped into the front pew. I found myself praying for strength, to be strong in front of the children.

Now, at this point, I ought to tell you that I considered myself a fairly religious person. Religious in the sense that, at the very least, I knew to pray in times of trouble.

Trouble had come to call frequently back then. Because of a downturn in the real estate market, Frank and I had just experienced severe financial difficulties, almost to the point of declaring bankruptcy. We had had four children in rapid succession; at one point we were the diaper-changers of a 3-year-old, a 2-year-old and newborn twins. At the age of three months, my only son, one of the twins, was diagnosed with Cystic Fibrosis.

It was also during all of this that Frank developed degenerative disc disease in his neck and underwent three separate cervical fusions, rendering him incapacitated for over a year. In addition, my own career was stalled for any number of reasons, not the least of which was probably my thoroughly depressing personal life.

And yet, throughout each of these obstacles, I felt as if my faith, my religion, would get me through. I had always known myself to be a strong person, and believed that I could handle any crisis, anything life wanted to shovel my way. I thought that if I did all the appropriate things, that is, kept my wits about me, stayed in positive focus and prayed, of course, in a sincere way, that I would prevail, that my life situation would improve.

What I hadn't planned on was my own downfall. My own health was never an issue, never a thought, never a fear. You see, I would go on. I could see anything through. I was the type of person who thought they could weather any storm, no matter how dark.

Until I was brought down. Until I sunk so low, so far in that dark abyss, that I no longer recognized the strong person who used to be me. Until I was nothing more than a bundle of terror, vomiting at the thought of dying. Within myself I raged indignantly, "I can't die; I'm young; I'm strong; I'm religious for God's sake! I'm trying to do the right thing; I'm working hard; I'm in the struggle. I am all of these things, so why is this happening?"

INITIAL DREAMS

Unless you happen to be Carl Jung or Sigmund Freud, dreams probably aren't of any interest to you. Like me, you laugh at their weirdness or summarily dismiss them as foolish. Before cancer, any credence I would have given to dreams would have been that they were my brain's way of "overnight batching" (a computer term) those events that I had not processed for some reason during the day. I may have been vaguely aware of a dream or two, but here again, they did not play any role whatsoever in my waking state. That was all about to change.

The first surgery removes the lump. Diagnosis – cancer. Within weeks, a second surgery removes all the lymph nodes from under my left arm. By comparing the total number of lymph nodes removed against the total number of lymph nodes involved, my doctors would make determination as to the intensity and duration of treatment. By now, I am really in the throes of it, trying to heal from both surgeries and prepare myself for whatever course of treatment is recommended.

The first dream:

I am running in the perimeter hallways of a huge building.
It has many sides, many corridors. A huge, impersonal building. I
think maybe it's the Pentagon. I am running down hallway after
hallway petrified. At some juncture, I pass in front of a set of

doors that are very cold and the cold, the dampness, is very threatening. My confusion and fear escalate. At some point, my mother is running along side of me. I attempt to explain this horrible fear to her when I again happen upon the same set of doors. Her eyes flash to me and simultaneously we mirror back to each other unspeakable terror.

I awake screaming. A week or so passes and a second dream occurs:

I am in my bedroom at home. I attempt to leave the room, but a sinister force envelopes me; darkness hovers around my head and prevents me from leaving. I try to scream, to resist, but the evil persists, sucking the air from my lungs.

I awake this time sweating and screaming. Days later, yet a third dream:

I am in my mother's bedroom in the home of my childhood. I am trying to leave the room. It is dusk. I can see the sun's last rays of day cast on my mother's bedroom wallpaper. I rush to the door, but, again, this dark presence envelopes me, violates me, sucks the air from my lungs. I gasp for breath, trying to scream for help. With my foot, I knock over a bedside lamp but no one hears it crash to the floor. I struggle to resist its hold.

Again, I awake screaming and extremely disoriented.

I do my best to ignore these dreams. I try desperately to dismiss them because they only serve to heighten my level of anxiety. Now, make no mistake, throughout this entire time I prayed religiously. I prayed every prayer I knew and then some. But praying did not ease my fear; these nightmares raged on.

Somewhere in the midst of all this angst, however, something strange occurred. It was early evening, mid-July. I had been barricaded in my bedroom all day, nursing my wounds, sleeping intermittently. I rolled over and hit the television switch just in time to see a program about a woman who had a near death experience. If I'm not mistaken, I believe the program was about the woman who wrote *Embraced by the Light*. I hadn't read her book, but hearing her story on television brought comfort to me. For some inexplicable reason, I remember feeling better. I think I finally faced the simple realization that everyone has to die – some before others. I felt I had reached a crossroad here. I finally stopped struggling with the notion of *dying*. I said aloud to myself, "Really Anne, how bad could it be?" Technically, the only thing bothering me was the not *living* part. Despite the fact that my mental framework could now grasp the concept of my death, it could not reconcile itself to forgoing a life not fully lived. Yet, somehow I drifted off to sleep feeling just a little less anxious.

Shortly thereafter, I had to go for a CAT scan because, with seven positive lymph nodes, my doctor worried that the cancer may have spread. This lovely procedure is particularly gruesome because it tracks where cancer had taken up additional space in my body, going on the hunt for more bad news, scoping out more places where my body had betrayed me. Physical pain would have been welcomed, compared to the mental anguish you endure while technicians do the virtual tour of your insides, searching the barrel of your body, looking in every crevice, behind every organ, for more of the unfortunate.

The morning of the CAT scan I awoke at dawn. I hadn't slept well for obvious reasons. But here it was 5:00 a.m. and I was fully awake, trembling slightly. I knelt by my bed and prayed. Prayed very hard and intently for good results. But I felt that I needed to make a larger effort, as if kneeling in that huddled mass beside my bed was not enough. I needed to make a more pronounced showing of my prayer. As if on cue, I felt like someone lead me downstairs, out the door and onto the lawn. I lay there in the early morning dew, face down, arms outstretched in my old pink nightgown, offering my life to God. I wanted Him to see me. To see me prostrate. My thought was to make my body a ground flag to heaven. To show Him that I was there, and that I was offering myself to Him.

As I lay there, my thoughts of control began to dissipate. I prayed that whatever He willed I would accept; I let control drain from my hands entirely. I lay there for another moment or so feeling the moist grass against the back of my hands and the beginning warmth of the new day's sun against my palms. I remember feeling a distinct sense of relief. It was okay to go on. It was the very thing I needed to do and once done, I started to feel better. Whatever happened from this point on was His Will.

✦ ✦ ✦

As it turned out, the CAT scan showed no evidence of metastases. But because of the number of cancerous lymph nodes – six nodes, (seven if you count the one removed from the first surgery), I was to receive 16 weeks of intense chemotherapy, followed by a daily dose of radiation for one month.

This was the Hopkins protocol for cases with over six cancer-ous lymph nodes. I had seven. So my thought was, *This is a good thing.* I am just barely over the mark, so to speak, but will receive the optimum amount of chemotherapy, an atomic blast to hope-fully annihilate any microscopic lingerers. I credit my oncologist, Dr. Diana Griffiths, for being so straightforward with me and also all of the nurses, in particular, Denise, for her warmth, sensitivity and humor during my treatments. I knew they were afraid for me. I could see it in their faces when my husband would pick me up after a treatment with four small kids in tow.

Losing my hair was the first outward sign that chemicals were violating my body. The nurses had promised that by the third week it would happen. Sitting at the kitchen table listening to my husband wrestle with the lawn mower in our back yard, I checked for the first signs of hair loss. I wondered if the nurses were right. I reached up and gave a slight tug. What my hand came back with was a paintbrush of hair. I was amazed and nauseous at the same time. A moment later, I was at the door yelling for Frank to "forget the lawn and come mow this!"

I'll admit that the first few chemo treatments were awful, but not for the obvious reasons. The vomiting stops and the exhaustion ebbs. But what I remember most was the smell of my body. It was as if I was rotting from the inside out. I would get wafts of this pungent odor, a combination of chemical and organic. A smell I had never known before, but obviously would never forget. Even now to write about it brings minor waves of nausea.

I think it's important to mention that I continued working. I went in as many days as I could muster. Secretly, I just wanted to stay hidden under the covers, but, in hindsight, being around other people kept my mind occupied. It gave me a reason to get up in the morning, make myself presentable: makeup, wig, etc. It kind of forced me to stay in the human race.

I also remember spending too much time in my bedroom, peering out my adjoining bathroom window in the late afternoon and hearing the sounds of children playing in the alley. Their laughter, their bikes, their big wheels. I heard the voices of my husband, neighbors, and other children. I felt so alone, so separated from them. I was on another planet. I wanted to be part of their world, but cancer kept me different. Cancer kept me hostage in my room. Everyone down there knew I had cancer. Everyone felt for me. But I couldn't take their pity, their stares, their fakeness or their fear. I especially couldn't take the sense of relief they felt when I wasn't around.

At this point I was still operating on automatic pilot. I would work those days that were good and sleep on those that weren't. I hadn't really dwelled too much on the future, the outcome of all this. I prayed and knew others were praying for me: my parents, all six of my brothers and sisters, my sister in laws, my friends, and in particular, my Aunt Stell.

I love my Aunt Stell. She's the closest our family has ever had to a living saint. From her home in Arizona, she prayed novenas and sent me a prayer for cancer patients. At first I laughed at the fact that there was actually an "official" prayer for cancer.

But each night and every morning I would include this prayer with the others and I would also pray whenever I experienced bouts of absolute terror. When I would again fully comprehend that this was happening to me. I had cancer. This was not a joke, a piece of gossip, a movie script, or someone else's trouble, this was wholly mine! And, somewhere in the depths of my being, I had to muster the strength to live with this fact, consciously and subconsciously.

It was the conscious part I had trouble dealing with. Because while you are busy following your medical instructions, nursing your wounds, flushing your portacath (a nifty little button like device placed in your chest to access your larger veins), having your blood drawn, trying to care for your children, keeping the persona going at work, checking your white blood cell count, figuring out dinner, groceries, (laundry,) you can find many avenues on which to sidetrack. You can very easily direct your focus solely on the mechanical part of your existence, even when you have cancer. *Especially* when you have cancer.

Somehow you can find a way to normalize even the most depressing features of cancer, make them part of your routine. If you are really good at it, you can actually pretend for a while that yours *is* the normal life. You can pretend that everyone has trouble cleaning their portacath and, for that matter, summer wigs don't do well on rainy days. It's no wonder that the steady stream of procedures and appointments can easily divert your attention from dealing with the more serious aspect of this disease. **The mechanical part of this disease can keep at bay the larger, looming question of whether you will live or die.**

+ + +

By now I am midway through my chemotherapy treatment and slowly regaining the use of my left arm, when one morning, sitting on the edge of my bed wrestling with a pair of panty hose, I gradually recalled a dream I had had the night before:

> *Frank and I are arguing about the color of a room in a*
> *beautiful big house. He's claiming the room was gray and I'm*
> *insisting that the room was white, a "glorious white," I said.*
> *There was dental moulding around a fireplace of which certain*
> *parts were painted a lovely soft shade of coral pink.*

I realized almost immediately that the room we were fussing over was the "living" room. There was a distinct emphasis on the word "living." As soon as my mind made that connection there was a powerful sensation, a rush of energy, for lack of a better term, throughout my entire body. In much the same powerful, unexplainable way my body had responded to the word "cancer" in the doctor's office, my body was now responding to the word "living." I now knew directly from this dream (feeling) that I was going to live. The room in my dream was a "glorious" shade of white. The color white symbolized Christ to me, the Resurrection. Pink represented areas of my body that were in the process of healing. The significance of this bizarre little dream was that it imparted to me a supreme sense of well being, a nearly physical expression of joy. Something wonderful had happened.

Within moments, the terrible dreams of the prior weeks now pushed their way to the forefront of my mind. They were beginning to make sense. Those dreams involved another pivotal room, the bedroom: my bedroom in the first dream, my mother's bedroom in the second. The bedroom symbolized sleep, eternal sleep. Death, fear. A pattern was emerging. These dreams communicated crucial messages to me. The me inside. The me I was unaware of until this moment. The one I never knew existed.

Then, there was a quiet excitement. A controlled sense of joy, a subdued energy. I was secretly harboring a most fantastic discovery. A wonderful connection to something unexplainable, an inner realm, some part of my being had just told me I was going to "live." A part of my being that had previously let me know that I had every right to be fearful. In those dreams of the bedroom, I was encountering a sleep, a death, something that threatened to take the very breath from my lungs.

And now, in retrospect, I realize that that first dream involved the hallways of a hospital, not the Pentagon. A huge impersonal building just the same, and those doors were the coldest doors in any hospital, the doors of the morgue. Who wouldn't experience uncontrollable fear at the thought of running down corridor after corridor only to be met by the doors to death?

Somehow, I knew then intrinsically in my being that I was going to live. The same intense knowing of cancer I had had before my diagnosis was now equally strong in convincing me that cancer would not take my life.

These dreams were so exciting to me. I told Frank and other family members immediately, and whoever else would listen. For the most part, my dream stories were met with lukewarm reactions and skepticism. People were not quite sure what I was babbling about; politely listening or suppressing yawns, but it made no difference to me. I was convinced I was on the mend. No one could quite grasp why I was so happy. How I could go to work brimming with excitement; just to be alive to connect with people every day. And while there were still moments when panic would stop me in my tracks, when I would remember that chemotherapy was pumping through my veins, the "living" room dream would return to refresh my spirit, to remind me that I was indeed going to live. This sequence of dreams became a constant source of comfort and reassurance to me and imparted a tremendous sense of wonder. I was smitten with my Self. My inner Self. There was no denying, no doubting their meaning. Each dream represented a part of the bigger picture, fitting into a perfectly patterned message tailored just for me. It was the best news I could have ever received.

The tremendous feeling of confidence imparted from these initial dreams was twofold. First, they introduced me to another part of me, my spirit, and secondly by their very nature convinced me firsthand that there really is something else going on. My life was not one-dimensional. That, in and of itself, certainly lessened the anxiety and fear of the unknown.

The euphoria from these dream experiences lasted the duration of my treatment. I recall only one exception to my sustained good humor. It was March. My last radiation treatment had ended a month earlier. I was trying to get to work, not feeling particularly well. My husband was recovering from his third neck surgery, all of the kids were sick, our '83 Caprice Wagon, affectionately dubbed "The Kermit Mobile" because of a bad paint job, was inoperable and I was waiting for a bus that never came. The March wind picked up and brought with it torrential rain. I ran for cover in the marble doorway of St. Mary's. The wind and rain were wreaking havoc on my summer wig, chilling my sparsely clad scalp. I remember half laughing, half crying, thinking I wasn't quite sure at this juncture what would have been better, to live through cancer or die! Because on that bitter cold March morning, it was a toss up!

PRECOGNITIVE DREAM

It is now several months after the last radiation treatment. It's Spring '93 and I am back to work full time. I am no longer sporting a wig, and my hair is growing back nicely. I am attempting to pick up my life where I left off, still reeling from the personal experience of those initial dreams when I encounter a totally different situation wrought from yet another dream.

I was sitting in my office about to call one of my closest friends, Susan B., when my phone rang. I picked it up and laughed. Who was on the other end? Susan B. Certainly not an uncommon experience. To think of someone only to hear from them a short time later. I mentioned to Susan that, for the past two nights, I had had dreams about people from my childhood named Susan. So it seemed logical to me that she was on my mind and that I should call her.

Normally, no one delves into someone else's dreams unless they are somehow involved. Let's face it – dreams are confusing enough to the dreamer, much less to someone else. Yet when I told Susan B. that for two nights running I was dreaming of Susans, she became uncommonly curious to know the nature of these dreams.

She pressed to know more and I countered with suggestions for lunch. I was really hungry and in no mood to detour over the long drawn-out details of dreams that I was sure were of no consequence to her. Yet she insisted. At this point I was becoming increasingly annoyed but I knew lunch was that much further away the longer I resisted. Relinquishing any notions of eating, I told her the dreams. The first was about "Miss Suzie," the mother of my childhood friend, Anne Bethe. Like me, Anne Bethe was the oldest of seven children and my best friend for many years. I had many fond memories of our great outdoor adventures on her farm. I actually didn't recall any part of the dream other than it was a very short dream about "Miss Suzie."

It had been probably a good 20 years since I had last seen Anne Bethe or Miss Suzie. My mother had learned of Miss Suzie's long battle with lung cancer and my only contact had been when paying my respects at the funeral home. I told this to Susan, but she still wasn't satisfied. Now she wanted to know about the second Susan dream. I continued to protest. "This is really stupid. What's the point of all this? You didn't know Miss Suzie; you're certainly not going to know the other Susan either. She, too, is from my childhood." I argued further, "You would have no way of knowing her. You grew up in Wales, on the other side of the world, and, furthermore, you are several years my senior. So, it really seems highly unlikely . . ." But it was no use; there would be no lunch plans until I gave up the second dream.

By then, I was famished. "Her name is Susan Edwards, okay?" And with that Susan exclaimed, "Anne, I know her!" My calm response was "No you don't. It's a common name. There's no way you know this girl from my eighth grade class at Our Lady of Perpetual Help in Ilchester, Maryland." Susan interrupted with, "Anne, yes, I do. She and her family relocated to Winchester, Virginia!"

I was dumbstruck. She did know her! My office chair spun a 360° while the hair on the back of my neck and arms stood at attention. It was a very uncanny feeling.

As it turned out, Susan had been briefly related by marriage to my friend's uncle and even though Susan later divorced him, she remained close with her ex-sister in law and her children, one of who was my little eighth-grade chum, Susan Edwards.

Still reeling from the fact that they actually knew each other I recounted the dream, remembering it vividly:

I felt as if I "flew" in to see Susan Edwards. She was standing in a line, perhaps at a blood bank, some place where you give or receive blood. I distinctly remember that I came right up to her and yelled out, "Susan! Hi! It's me, Anne Marie! How are you? Why you look exactly the same!" Which she did. She was just as I remembered her. Medium length, very blonde hair, parted slightly to the side. I marveled how she hadn't changed at all since our childhood days. I was so excited to see her. She was holding what appeared to be a newborn infant. I congratulated her and asked to see the child. She uncovered the blanket revealing a sweet baby boy with dark hair. This really surprised me because Susan had such blonde hair, a real towhead. I left with the distinct impression that something was not quite right because they were standing in a line, a bloodline.

That was the dream. Susan was very quiet on the other end of the phone. Finally she said, "Let me call my former sister-in-law and find out if Susan ever got pregnant. I know that she and her husband had been trying unsuccessfully for many years. I'll call you right back." And with that she hung up.

Within 10 minutes she was back on the phone with me. She had spoken with her ex-sister in-law and confirmed that Susan Edwards had indeed given birth to a baby boy with dark hair some three weeks earlier in Houston, Texas. Mother and child were doing well; little John, as he was named, had Down Syndrome!

What was this dream, a coincidence? I couldn't make any sense of it. Having a friend in common with a friend from 30 years ago is somewhat unusual, but that could almost be explained away by the "it's a small world" theory. But the dream itself, her likeness, her baby and the sense of something out of order, that just convinced me that this was no coincidence. As a matter of fact, that's when I started thinking that perhaps there are no such things as coincidences. I told everyone I knew. I weaved this story into dozens of conversations, hoping someone could offer some plausible explanation. For a while I even entertained the idea that this was something that happened to people when they received too much chemotherapy, that somehow it heightens your sense of communication or awareness. (Maybe the chemo didn't, but the cancer did.) I didn't know what to think! Yet no one could convince me that any part of that story was a coincidence.

The fact that the two Susans were related alone convinces me that we are all interconnected at some level. The fact that the details of the dream so closely resembled reality produced feelings similar to those I felt the morning of the "living room dream" Exhilaration, grace, a flow of kinetic energy.

This event became an untiring source of amusement and amazement to me. To this day, I am unsure as to why it occurred. This precognitive episode culminated almost a year later when I had an opportunity to re-meet Susan Edwards and be introduced to her dear son. She was as amazed as I. Neither one of us had ever thought about the other since our days as two of the 20 or so eighth-graders at Our Lady of Perpetual Help. It should also be noted that she looked exactly as she did in the dream. As of this writing, both she and her son are doing well. I usually receive a card at Christmas.

EMBRACE YOUR FEAR

It is now probably a year later and I am standing on the landing to the second floor, laundry basket in hand, crying. Crying because even though I thought I was cured, even though I wanted to believe with all my heart that this was over, that I could now put it all behind me like a bad dream, I cannot shake this awful dread, this constant nagging of a reoccurrence.

As with any trauma, while you're in the throes of it, you concentrate on one thing and one thing only: surviving. But then, when you go on living, the thought that you had cancer, and that cancer could return, become unrelentingly presence in your life.

I would go every few months for my checkups, continue with my usual routine. And that was the problem; I was trying to do exactly what I did before all this happened. I was trying to get back to the way life was before cancer. I didn't like this change.

The irony here is that I have always been a big advocate for change. I was one of those people who thrived on change and changed all the time. Change for change's sake. Changed jobs, changed procedures at work, changed hairstyles, wallpaper, furniture. You name it, I'd find a reason to change it.

And now, as someone who loved change, I had to admit that

there was one change I hated. This change in my medical history. This change in how I viewed myself, my own mortality, my living with the fear of cancer for the rest of my life. I grew to hate the undeniable change in my status. How long did I have? What were the chances of reoccurrence? Any new development meant that my life could take an amazing "change" for the worse. How do you live day in and day out with that hanging over your head?

So I tried to reset all the blocks straight. I reentered the planet called home, inhabited by family and friends, I returned to work full time. My hair grew back nicely. Shouldn't my life do the same? There was only one problem. What was to keep that bolt of cancer from striking me again?

These thoughts hovered in the background of my mind, leaving me feeling terribly depressed. Again, it was the resurgence of that old control issue. How could I ever be in control of my life again? I worried every time I felt a muscle ache, was unexplainably tired, or had the flu. Every time I received a donation request from the American Cancer Society I would plummet downward. Sending them a check, I mentally bargained, would stave off any cellular action in my body.

It seemed as if every other month was October again. National Breast Cancer Month. Cancer Awareness everywhere. For a while it seemed like everyone I knew knew someone who had just been diagnosed, and somehow this information found its way to me like a heat-seeking missile. When, I agonized, would I ever feel comfortable living with this undeniable fact, the fact that I was now one of the many, unforgivable, irresolvable, non-insurable cancer statistics?

The answer came in the following dream:

I am having a huge cocktail party, entertaining everyone I know: family, friends, business associates, everyone in my life. The walls of my home are all glass, with glass doors everywhere. The house itself is situated in an isolated part of downtown Baltimore, a non-residential area off the Expressway.

Everyone is laughing, carrying on, drinking, and having a great time. I, on the other hand, am constantly checking the windows and doors, making sure they stay shut. But guests are milling in and out, ignoring my requests to shut the doors. I am clearly distressed and cannot enjoy my own party. In an instant, I realize my vigilance has failed. Whatever I was trying to keep out had made its way in. Hovering darkness was now whirling around me, above me. I screamed for someone to call the police, to get some help, but everyone continued to party, totally oblivious to my rantings.

This darkness was now at my mother's china closet and had caused all of her china to come crashing in pieces to the floor. It was as if this darkness were a child having a temper tantrum. At that moment, I realized that the only one who was going to stop this insanity was I. I had to stop this thing before it ruined everything I held dear. So I reached for it, wrestled it to the ground, wrapped my arms around it and began softly chiding it in a loving manner, as you would an errant child. Gently scolding it for behaving so badly. I was actually killing it with kindness. Somehow I knew, then, that was the only way to calm it down and have it behave normally.

I awoke instantly.

By then, I had begun to recognize some of the signs of significant dreaming. Significant dreaming occurs when you are jolted awake, fully conscious, remembering the dream with absolute clarity. It's as if one moment you are deeply asleep, and the next your eyes are wide open, your mind as sharp as after that third cup of coffee.

The last part of the dream lingered: *I reached for it, wrestled it to the ground, wrapped my arms around it and began softly chiding it in a loving manner, as you would an errant child. Gently scolding it for behaving so badly. I was actually killing it with kindness. Somehow I knew, then, that was the only way to calm it down and have it behave normally.*

Upon awakening, two words hung in the forefront of my mind: "love" and "fear." I worked through the dream in sections.

The first part of the dream depicts my life and how vulnerable I felt, evidenced by the many glass windows and glass doors. The fact that my house was situated in a remote area emphasized the isolation felt by people with cancer. Another detail of the dream was that my house was located on a lot that, in real life, houses the Maryland State Penitentiary, illustrating so well the feelings of imprisonment and separation that accompanied my fear of a reoccurrence.

The next scene in the dream depicted everyone enjoying the party of life – everyone except me. I was preoccupied with shutting something out, making sure that the windows and doors stayed closed. The people in my life could not understand or fathom my anxiety. They were unable to rescue me from my own fear. And this fear I attempted to keep outside was the fear of cancer's return. Despite my many desperate efforts to keep it at bay, to shut it out of my "world," it had made its way back into my life.

Like a storm gaining momentum, once on its path, fear of cancer's return had the potential to ruin everything I valued, symbolized in the dream by my mother's china. It would wreak a path of destruction if I did not actively choose to face it head on. In the dream, I made the conscious choice to confront and embrace that which threatened to destroy me. The innate ability is there. I had to recognize the fear for what it was and understand its nature. As in the dream, just as a parent loves its child, so too can a person learn to cradle fear in the arms of love.

There, again, was the phenomenal power of a dream to help me cope with my conscious life. I would replay the details of that message over and over in my head. It all made sense to me, despite the fact that it was a very difficult idea to accept, to understand, much less incorporate into my daily life. There are only two modalities of living. Living out of love; living out of fear. So, in essence, the dream was telling me that I had to learn to love what I feared the most, I had to learn to love the experience, and the personal growth that was occurring as a result of cancer. It has only been over time that I can honestly say that I have done this.

The BIG DREAM

It is now the summer of 1995. For nearly two years I had tormented myself with the idea of leaving my job, and soon I came to the realization that I could no longer sit in my downtown office and shuffle papers from one side of my desk to the other. For 12 years, I steadily climbed the ladder in a specialty insurance company. It seemed as if all I did was wait for a meeting, call a meeting or attend a meeting. "Let's do lunch" was the highlight of my day.

It became patently clear that my 12 years there had been devoted to honing the skills of an extraordinarily proficient corporate puppet; a fairly effortless way to knock down a healthy salary and benefits. Unfortunately, as much as I tried to infuse my job with meaning, it was useless. I was exhausted, spending eight hours every day working at being useless. I had outgrown my position, but I also felt that my philosophy on life had taken a sharp left. I didn't want to be hermetically sealed in that building any longer than I had to.

So, much to Frank's chagrin, I quit my job. Of course I understood his uneasiness. I had always worked; to not work was not on our menu of options. Frank is a builder by trade, an excellent one at that. Actually, Frank was *born* a builder. His innate passion to understand how things work; how things come together, the excitement he feels bringing a building up out of the ground makes him more artist than businessman. By that I mean if he is going to put his name on something it has to be right, it has to be the way he wants it, even if it means pulling the extra money out of his pockets, out of his profits. And so for as long as I have known him, his business plan is to build. It's what he loves to do and does so well.

Building is a risky business so we always relied on both of our incomes, mine more so for the benefits and stability it provided. Especially in light of my stint with cancer, and our son's chronic health problems, Frank didn't relish the idea of running solo out there. Yet the whole idea of being tied to a useless, meaningless job over the notion of "benefits" drove me crazy. Talk about imprisonment. The longer I stayed, the more I felt like one of those big cats at the zoo, incessantly prowling my cement floor, rubbing up against the wrought iron cage, over and over again, every day, wondering how much longer can I do this. I mean what was I doing anyway? I was protecting my sorry butt, purely for the sake of "just in case." Just in case what? In case cancer returned.

In one afternoon, I negotiated a package with my boss and threw caution to the wind. I left my job of 12 years, benefits and all! It was time for me to drop this road and chart a new course. My revised life plan was to tighten the money belt, to be a stay-at-home mom (a luxury I hadn't afforded myself until that point), and to help Frank with his business.

It was a wonderful feeling to be home full time, to take the kids to the pool, plan nice dinners, have the beds made and the house in some type of order for the first time ever. Frank's business grew steadily. And, as a small company, we were able to secure a good health insurance plan for our family, which covered our son's pre-

existing condition and the proverbial skeleton in my health closet
– cancer.

It took awhile to become accustomed to "house" life. But it was
what I wanted. I no longer felt divided between family and career.
The ego issues of being "somebody" were then replaced with calls for
"mom's help," homemade cupcakes, hours of laughter and content-
ment as the full time natural custodian of my kids. I also learned
to relax for the first time. The squealing metal tracks of a 5:00 a.m.
Metro to New York were replaced with squealing kids at the neigh-
borhood pool. I was a little shell-shocked initially; I wasn't prepared
for the onslaught of children and mothers that descend upon the
pool like a herd of elephants the first week school lets out. I also felt
somewhat awkward. I was a stranger in a strange land. Who would I
talk to? What would we talk about? I could talk a blue streak about
Quality Assurance Issues on some new product line, but I didn't
have a clue which grocer was running the sale on boneless chicken.
Before I left my job, we had just initiated casual day on Friday. *What
is acceptable dress now?* I panicked. I had never done this before,
other than on the weekends, and we both know where my weekends
were spent – laundry!

Happily though, I adjusted. The year passed, the kids were
doing well, I was busy running a household, making new friends,
helping Frank with his business, loving life.

It wasn't until one night in the Fall of '97 that the dreams started again. I had fallen to sleep as normal. Only three hours later, I sat
straight up in bed yelling "Bunky!" with absolutely no recollection
of any dream. Instinctively, though, I knew that I was calling out the
name of a dog of my former roommate and close friend of nearly
20 years earlier. I barely remembered what the dog looked like, but

I knew his name was "Bunky." Now *that* was one item of my life's minutia that I certainly would not have remembered in my conscious state, even if you put a gun to my head. And yet I was jolted awake when the name 'Bunky' bounced like a basketball against the side of my brain. I sat there for a minute or so, in a befuddled state, scratching my head, muttering "Bunky, Bunky," and with a muffled sigh, I swiftly returned to my sleep state.

The very next night, I again dreamt about a dog. But this dream was unlike the dream of the night before. This was a dream about the four-legged love of my life, my best friend, my constant companion, my confidant, soul mate, consoler, and my greatest fan – Günter. Given to me by my first husband this dog was by my side for 17 years. A Norwegian elkhound mix, with big ears and spindly legs, he was the only redeeming asset of my short-lived first marriage. He adored me and I adored him. He accompanied me through my divorce, my crazy single years, my second marriage, the birth of all my children, three moves, and all our medical maladies. It was Günter who never left my side while I struggled with cancer. When I slept all day and all night he would too, always there at my feet or nestled close on my bed, our backs back to back.

I remember, even in his final years, he would jump excitedly to see me coming home from work. He was always happy to be with me. And then one day he decided to leave. It was a year or so after my last treatment. He stopped eating and wouldn't get up. Frank said he dreaded the day Günter would die, because he predicted I would be a basket case. But in actuality I was fine with it. It was all right; I understood that it was his time. And so to the dream:

I am sitting in a small craft on a lake or a very calm river.

I look over and see Günter by my side. I am ecstatic to see him. I lovingly exclaim "Günter! It's you! You're here!" And in a split second he has moved away from me and there is water between us.

I call to him and before my eyes he transforms into an immense beam of light, emitting absolute joy, radiant warmth, powerful surges of extreme love. Indescribable feelings, feelings beyond any sensory perception I have ever felt. It left me breathless, spellbound, motionless and emotional. Every exquisite feeling I have ever had all forged into one unearthly powerful moment.

Completely awake, I lay there on my back, still with wonderment. Dreams of dogs. Dogs. Two distinct references to dog. Then *Dog is God spelled backward.* And with that thought, a tingling sensation encased my body as if to say, "Yes!"

Is this what God feels like? The most powerful, most profound, most peaceful pull on the very pulse of my being; on the center of my soul. A nearly physical rush of feeling with the force of the entire universe surging through my center.

I have only the memory of it. I cannot duplicate the experience. It is near impossible to describe with words. It felt like an atomic burst beyond love. It transcends anything I have ever experienced before in my life. The hauntingly pleasurable memory of this dream was nearly undone by a seemingly devastating dream only two weeks later.

It is now November. I find myself up in the middle of the night taking care of one of the kids. And, upon returning to bed, I knew, as any experienced mother would, that it might take some time getting back to sleep. So, as I lay there waiting for sleep, I began thinking about my life. I guess you could say I was thinking about life's most profound question, one that I had never officially asked before, but certainly one that had played over in my mind many times before. Especially in light of my bout with cancer some four years earlier, it seemed as if these words finally wanted to form on my lips. "What is my purpose in life?" "Why am I still here?"

Tossing and turning, I decided on what I thought was the right answer. My purpose, I concluded, was to be a dedicated, loving wife and mother; this was the reason why I was still here. Feeling fairly confident in my assessment, I drifted off to sleep. Only to dream the following:

Frank and I enter a rehabilitated house in Federal Hill in Baltimore. It appears to be the home in which we used to live. I immediately notice that the workmanship is very shoddy on the inside. The exterior looks rehabbed, but the interior is in poor shape. I become tense and fearful. I want to back out, to leave. But at someone's insistence we continue through. Once inside, I am immediately drawn to a room in the back, perhaps the kitchen and yet it isn't a kitchen but a beautiful room with a huge bay window with many divided lights.

Beyond the window is an exquisite garden, with every flower imaginable. The sky is elegant, colored in surreal paint. It is a wonderful scene. Upon seeing this, my whole demeanor changes. I am no longer fearful, but relaxed, refreshed, ready to explore the rest of the house. I climb the stairs to see what's above and as I do so, I notice the steps become increasingly gritty with layers of dirt and cracked linoleum.

Midway up the stairs, I can see, for lack of a better word, many souls. They are lifeless, formless, pale gray figures with eyes. Eyes with empty stares. These souls were on the second floor in the bedroom area. There was also a large window on this level of the house along side these lifeless forms. Outside the window, the surroundings were a murky gray-green, the color of swamp and moss. It possibly could have been underwater. Perhaps even a sewer.

At this precise moment a voice cut through this image and in a calm, matter of fact, almost rhetorical manner stated, "Don't you think you should be doing research in lymphoma? After all, you were a million to one, your cancer was perfect, the best, of the highest order."

Heart pounding, I spun out of bed, stopping in the hallway only to gasp for breath, scarcely hearing, much less understanding, what was said, where it came from and from whom it was spoken!

Those powerful words rocked my entire being, shocked my soul or that part of me that is so inner I only realize it is there when I am on the other end of a gun barrel, falling through the sky at 30,000 feet or listening to a stranger in a long white jacket politely tell me I have cancer!

Who in the world would say such a thing to me and say it chidingly, like it was something I should have already known. This whole matter bordered on the preposterous. And why a reference to lymphoma? Who ever said lymphoma? I had breast cancer! Granted, it was never found in the breast, just in the lymph nodes, but what does that mean? And the word "research." Somebody definitely has the wrong guy, I failed chemistry in junior year. I never opened the book!

"A million to one?" Yeah right, like I'm the only person out there who's had cancer. And another thing, how can "cancer" be perfect, the best, of the highest order or form or whatever the hell was said? That's an oxymoron if I ever heard one. Perfect cancer. Why, that's like saying perfect death, perfect fear, perfect torture. Perfect hell on earth! No. There's no way any of this makes sense. This is a gross mistake. Just a bad dream. This has to be ignored. Something must have been lost in the translation here. This was no dream, I must have been hallucinating!

And so there was an absolutely outrageous answer to what I thought was a seemingly harmless question, a question I hadn't really intended to ask. I mean it's not like this was some hot burning issue in my life! It's not like it was the dark night of my soul. I was just trying to get back to sleep. I could have been counting sheep for that matter. I was bored, I was only kidding, I didn't want to know what to do with my life; really, my life was fine the way it was. I already knew what to do.

All of these thoughts and more raced through my mind. I couldn't think clearly. Meanwhile, was I losing my mind? Was all of this some freakish nightmare? It took two torturous days before I worked up enough courage to even repeat this to anyone, even Frank.

I knew Frank would immediately think something was wrong, that cancer had come back or that, as I suspected, I was losing my mind. He was worried, but at least he had the presence of mind to find a mild sedative in our medicine cabinet so I could sleep. Because after that dream, sleep was not something I relished. I didn't know what to do or where to turn. Yet, I couldn't ignore this horrific dream. On the one hand, how could I value so dearly all the other dreams, and at the same time dismiss this one as some type of aberration. Of course I couldn't. So I had to accept this dream without understanding any part of it.

My frame of mind was not good. The sedatives stopped working. I was a nervous wreck, I couldn't think straight. I knew I had to talk to someone. I was very fearful and, with such a strong Catholic background, I was heavily leaning on the notion that the dream meant that I was somehow to be sacrificed for the common good, maybe some sort of medical experiment. Or worse yet, that I really was losing my mind, that I was on the verge of becoming one of the religiously insane. So at Frank's insistence, I contacted an old friend, Fr. Chris, a Jesuit priest.

I first met Chris in my sophomore year at a small, Catholic girls' high school in Ilchester, Maryland. Chris was young, handsome and dynamic, which contributed to his popularity among the entire student body. He was our religious instructor, confessor and guidance counselor. During the tumultuous times of the late '60s, he stressed the need to think independently. He taught us above everything else, to think for ourselves, not to be led like lambs.

After high school, our paths crossed only a few times: after the sudden, tragic death of one of our dearest classmates and then at a series of weddings, one of which was mine. It had been quite a few years since I had last seen him.

Within two days, I was seated across from Chris trying my best to explain, between emotional outbursts, a condensed version of what had been going on – the cancer, the dreams, my revised life plan, etc. He listened intently and even affirmed my dream experiences with one of his own.

He had been offered a prominent position within the Jesuit hierarchy and before giving his decision he went home and slept on it. That night he had an intensely personal dream that led him to make another choice – a choice to leave the Jesuits and become a parish priest. Today he is the popular pastor at a very large congregation in Baltimore County, touching many lives with his magnetic and engaging personality as well as his inspiring sermons.

So after listening nearly an hour or so to my chaotic ranting, he paused for what seemed like an eternity and then said very succinctly "Well, Anne Marie, evidently God spared you for a reason."

Now to many people this generic response may seem like a logical thing for a priest to say. This is part of a priest's repertoire of pat answers to life's dilemmas. But such a thought had never occurred to me. I never thought that God was personally involved in this, or that He deliberately chose me for something, or that He even knew who I was.

It took a while for this idea to sink in. But by the time I left Chris's office, I was walking across the parking lot in the rain and feeling a complete and utter sense of exhilaration, joy and specialness. I was spared for a reason. It was beginning to take shape like the positive part of the Catholic experience, like all the stories I had read as a child. "The Lives of the Saints," of St. Catherine Laboure, Maria Goretti, St. Martin dePorres. Again, I was full of wonder and excitement. Could Fr. Chris possibly be right? How could he say that? Did he mean it? Could I accept such an explanation? In any event, it worked. I stopped fretting and did as he suggested. "Stay open and let things unfold, stop worrying and keep track of your dreams. Write them down."

Over the next few weeks, messages would wake me suddenly

from sleep. Not exactly dreams, more like one-liners. They usually occurred in the early morning hours just before dawn. A thought would wake me. It would just be there, waiting to be acknowledged. The first was the simple statement, "God loves you," which is pretty self-explanatory. Then there was another one, which I just caught the tail end of "Helping you say goodbye (pause) . . . Something from Arizona."

This one gave me some cause for alarm. *Helping me say goodbye?* I fretted. *Where am I going? Why do I need to say goodbye?* I had relatives in Arizona – my sister, my Aunt Stell. At the time, I didn't quite understand what this meant. But I remembered Fr. Chris's instructions so I took to writing everything down. This helped me feel as if I was somehow actively participating in the process.

Within a few weeks of this dream, I unwittingly adopted my Aunt Stell's dog. She was planning to move back East and needed someone to house him temporarily until she got settled. That someone would be me. After the first of the year, I got the call to pick up my 40-pound parcel at the airport. a mixed, black and white terrier/spaniel named Pudge or Pugs, I never was quite sure. And while my beloved Aunt died before making it back to Baltimore, our relationship continued through my care of Pugs over the next few years.

In many small ways, he reminded me of my dear aunt. He sported a tiny tuff of soft gray hair on the very top of his head. This hair was the same color and texture as Aunt Stell's. He also tended to softly snore, as she would do so many nights while we watched "Gunsmoke" in her third floor apartment. When Pudge passed on I was able to mourn the passing of my Aunt in a more final way. The last little bit of Stell was gone now. As stated in the dream, caring for Pudge did in fact "help me say goodbye," did help me say all my special goodbyes to Aunt Stell, in ways that could not be accomplished with a brief trip to the Intensive Care Unit of a Phoenix Hospital. For this I am very grateful.

✦ ✦ ✦

Guidance and inspiration were coming, then, in all different forms: symbolic dreams, precognitive dreams, verbal suggestions and yes, even songs.

The next message came from a song by The Supremes:

Someday we'll be together.
You're far away from me, my love,
But just as sure now, now baby as there are stars above,
Some day we'll be together

I should mention that when I receive these messages, I experience a whole body sensation, a surge of excitement. If I were a car, I would classify this feeling as passing gear. This wave of confirmation awakens my spirit, my soul. It is a physical way of verifying that I understand the meaning of the message. If my initial thoughts are inaccurate, I don't receive that flush of feeling. So, you see, it then becomes a brief exercise in processing the message until I receive that strong "ah ha" feeling. Then I know I am on the right track.

"Someday we'll be together" became a deep source of comfort and amusement to me. Comfort because the very essence of the lyrics speaks to me of a Divine plan of love and ultimate union and wholeness. Amusement that pop lyrics of the '60s would be used to communicate with me. But then why not? I've had a radio glued to my ear since I was 11 years old. Why not use the very medium I love and with which I am so familiar.

A few days later another song awakens me around 2:30 a.m.

I'm coming out, I want the world to know
Got to let it show, I'm coming out
There's so much more to me, Show the world all my
    abilities;
I think this time around, I am going to do it
Like you never knew it;
I have to make them understand
I've got it well in hand
And oh how I have planned
There is no need to fear,
I feel so good every time I hear
I'm coming out.

Years ago, these were just catchy words I mindlessly mouthed while cruising in my mother's sedan. That particular night, the words changed into a much more personal message. The real me was emerging, the me that listens to an inner voice, not the voice of a parent, a husband, a boss, a girlfriend, a stranger, a child. I am connecting to a new source, a source that will lead me to the life I am meant to live. This was an opportunity to reveal my true abilities, my real potential, to spread my wings and fly fearlessly – it's a great feeling. It's a great song!

In early December, 1997, a few weeks after the last of my "music messages," a new dream occured:

I am flying around a city at night. (If I had to guess I would say the city is Hartford, Connecticut – a city where Frank and I had occasion to stay while visiting his daughter at college.) It is very dark. The only lights are very faint street-lights. But I am actually flying, experiencing an incredible feeling of weightlessness, power, speed and total exhilaration. I am aware of someone lightly clinging to my back, their fingertips gently resting on my shoulders. It seems as if I am transporting someone. I am carrying them on my back. I lead this person through a labyrinth of back streets and dark alleys. We are hovering just above the city lights, maybe twenty feet or so. We have an aerial view of everything. At some point, this person starts to slide off my back, fingertips slipping from my shoulders. There is a dark figure below waiting in a dimly lit alley, as if to prey on this person once he or she falls.

To prevent this from happening, I increase my thrust and speed, feeling the power of jet engines. I take off and level out, safely securing my charge once again on my back. I continue the journey with a tremendous sense of ease and confidence, somehow knowing our destination.

Upon waking, a sense of pure, authentic power and confidence lingered. What a wonderful dream. My initial thought was that I would be guiding someone through an ordeal of fear; in all likelihood, I expected it to be someone with cancer, someone who needed my help. I felt that this dream very clearly illustrated my shouldering a responsibility for this unknown person, guiding them on this journey. This seemed to be a very simple, straightforward assignment – one I actually considered myself capable of doing. And so, for the next few months, I waited in earnest for that "someone" to enter my life.

Later I realized that this dream had been interpreted a little too literally. There was a much deeper meaning and benefit to this dream, one that I continue to interpret even now.

Early January, 1998, this dream grabs my gut:

I am visiting a friend, Salli. There are many cats. Dozens of them circle my feet and, at once, several jump up and dig their claws into my back. It is very painful. I wince and at once my oncologist is there to administer a shot for pain, which I refuse. "It's too late, the pain is already here."

I awake suddenly, confused by this dream. Repeatng the word cat, cat, cat. But nothing. Then cat, cat, CAT scan. Just the words "CAT scan!" I cannot deny the whole body sensation I experienced. Like the dreams before, I felt the rippling of energy throughout my body, resonating from the center of my chest.

I am now terribly confused by this dream. A CAT scan. Yes, I am familiar with CAT scans. But what does it mean?. I keep this dream to myself, but I write it down and try to stay open. It's very hard. I am frightened again. Within the next day or so, this thought is voiced to me in the early morning hour as I awake; "There is a shadow on your bladder; but it will be flushed out." Silence. Then the word "saccharine."

I nose dive into my own personal panic, piecing together a truly frightening scenario. With buckets of fear and negativity, I paint the picture of a new cancer: lymphoma, appearing in my bladder, and the need for a CAT scan.

Clearly, I had to act and act quickly. I told my oncologist the nature of these recent weighty dreams about research in lymphoma, coupled with the CAT scan message and shadow on my bladder. For me there was only one explanation. Something was terribly wrong and it needed attention. I credit my doctor for not totally blowing me off. She was very sympathetic and offered her total support. She assured me that there were plenty of medical mysteries she had personally witnessed for which there were no plausible explanations.

After running a bunch of preliminary tests, all of which proved negative, I still wanted a CAT scan, even at my own expense. I had reversed my thinking; again, I was operating under the negative Catholic notion of self-sacrifice. As a young and voracious reader of the "Lives of the Saints," how could I not fashion the idea that cancer had metastasized to the bladder and I was to be some sort of medical sacrifice? Researchers would use me to experiment in the treatment of lymphoma, or something like that.

My imagination was really in overdrive. The going was really going to get tough. This was how God was showing His "love" for me. Except I didn't really think I was up to the task! I wanted to live. True, I didn't fear dying (as much) but, hey, there was still a whole lot of living I wanted to do.

In my panic stricken state, I insisted on a CAT scan. What I remember of that day, the day I had the CAT scan, was that I again surrendered my will to God. I was totally convinced that something would show up on the scan and that I must stay open to whatever it was.

I remember sitting in the waiting room reading a book I had actually given my husband as a Christmas present, *Anatomy of the Spirit*, by Carolyn Myss. We had been surfing the television channels and happened upon a PBS Special about her work in energy medicine. Frank and I were immediately drawn to what she was presenting and so I ordered the book. And, as with most self-help books, I'm the only one who ends up reading them.

Midway through the book, one passage caught my eye concerning St. Francis of Assisi and his prayer "Lord, make me an instrument of your peace." At once I felt that whole body feeling. Calmness again enveloped me. I was prepared for the results, whatever the outcome.

As it turned out, there was nothing there except a few kidney stones, which were perfectly normal for someone my age.

So what was the meaning of this exercise, this fiasco of fear? Even now I wonder. I subscribe to the notion that everything in life happens for a reason. So as I write, three purposes come to mind. The first and most pivotal, perhaps, is that this was another exercise in "surrendering," another opportunity to remember who is in charge of my life (not that I had forgotten). The second purpose was to more fully understand the meaning of "instrument of your peace." Perhaps I again needed to find myself in the throes of panic and fear and remember who and what had saved me before. And the third message was to stop using saccharine. (Unbeknownst to me at that time, there were studies evidently linking the excessive use of saccharine with bladder cancer.)

Now, I am beginning to notice that often, if not always, these dreams occur in groups. The first, perhaps, as a precursor to the next. For example in the dream where I am flying around Hartford, Connecticut, I had concluded that I would be helping someone else, that I would be supporting another person. I guess I was half right. What if that person I am carrying is me, my Self? What if this is a demonstration of how "my spirit" will guide me through the labyrinth, that I will "slip" in fear, but that my "spirit" is leading me, confident in its role.

I questioned what the city of Hartford meant in the dream. Hartford represents insurance companies to me; I had known that at one time Hartford was the hub of insurance companies. Why was I flying above Hartford? Maybe to symbolize that this journey is above all that, much more lofty in nature and that there is a purpose to all of this. I don't know my destination, but I do feel the confidence now of that dream. I do feel I am being guided. I am being led.

So perhaps the flying dream occurred in combination or in preparation for the second, more frightening dream. Perhaps it had to happen this way; I had to revert to that place of terror to again experience the necessity of surrender. And perhaps I also needed to be personally introduced to the notion of "instrument of your peace," and the idea that part of my journey might include that role.

I got over the secondary scare-episode and continued recording my dreams. I also began revealing the incredible dream experiences I was having to people other than my husband.

During these few months, I remember being keenly aware of life's excitement. I was like a can of shaken soda; show the slightest bit of interest in my dreams, and story after story would effervesce uncontrollably to whoever would listen.

At a basketball practice, I recounted to my close friend, Beth, the "Big Dream," the lymphoma research dream, when she turned to me and said, "Sounds like you need to read Jung. You need to get a hold of the works of Carl Jung."

Within a matter of days, I was immersed in *Memories, Dreams and Reflections*. Having never read Jung before, I was encouraged by his recollection of dreams and life experiences and his theories on both; I began to see similarities in the symbolism of his dreams and my own. I came to recognize synchronicities, intuition and the whole notion of the collective unconscious. I suppose, in retrospect, I was beginning to "awaken." I was awakening to a new level of life, a level that was so much deeper – richer with meaning, feeling, and emotion. I had graduated to a level where I began to look past the obvious, to look beyond the apparent, to see people and situations in a new light. I began to understand that all of my experiences were important to my growth and learning. I began to look at others as part of me. I tried and still try to remember that I cannot walk their paths; that I cannot judge their lives, that they, too, have their own journeys, their own ways to awaken.

From all outside appearances, I was still just a mother of four, working with her husband, making a life in Baltimore. But on the inside things were happening, feelings were jelling. Life was taking on a higher level of pure fun. pure exuberance. I would sit in traffic and wonder who else among the rows of morning beltway zombies was experiencing this keen sense of awakening, this new discovery about life. I looked to connect with anyone who expressed even the slightest interest in dreams, or in this heightened sense of consciousness.

In mid-February, 1998, another song enters my dream state and awakens me. This one I just barely know. It's Arlo Guthrie's "City of New Orleans," and these words softly followed: "Be creative." I was stumped. I had been to New Orleans on business years before and loved the city. Was that it? Nothing – no feelings surfaced. So I waited.

Within a few days my former neighbor, a research doctor at Hopkins, happened to call for my husband. I answered the phone.

We talked briefly and she remembered hearing about my newfound interest in cancer. She told me about an upcoming meeting at Hopkins addressing alternative approaches to medicine. My interest peaked, so she faxed over the details.

Then the message became clear. A major part of Hopkins Medical campus borders on "Orleans" Street in Baltimore. "Be creative." Okay, so I had to stretch a little to get this one. Intuitively, I knew that I should attend this conference.

In March, I found myself attending a two-day seminar, entitled "Bridging the Gap between Conventional and Alternative Medicine." Quite frankly, through the first half of the first day I couldn't for the life of me figure out why I was there. I tried to stay open and attentive, listening to presentations on everything from auryvedera to Tai Chi, homeopathic remedies to biofeedback, but I was becoming somewhat discouraged. All morning and most of the afternoon, there had been nothing that seemed even remotely interesting to me. I started wondering why I was there. Was this a mistake? Was this an entire waste of time?

I was debating whether to sneak out early and get a jump on traffic, when the next speaker stood up and immediately began talking about the ancient Greek practices involving healing baths and inducing the sick to *dream*. I immediately sat up with rapt attention. I was overwhelmed when he stated so succinctly that which I had been unable to describe until that moment. "The time has come for conventional medicine and spirituality to merge." That was it! The word was "spirituality." That was what I had been missing. That was what had eluded me! Until that moment, I had been describing my experiences with dreams as a Mind/Body connection, never quite satisfied with the explanation. Because in actuality, it is much more than mind/body – it is spirit!

I was overcome with emotion. I couldn't hear anything but my own heart pounding out of control. I couldn't hold back tears. In the subdued hush of that greyly lit auditorium, the doctor finished speaking and there was what seemed to be an interminable space of absolute silence, an emotional pause that unified every person in that audience. Then a rush of applause.

When the lights went up, I was relieved to see that I wasn't the only person brought to tears by what this man had said. Here, at one of the world's leading health institutions, an institution devoted to the science of medicine, was a doctor announcing that science alone is not the answer, that only the combination of spirituality and medicine brings whole, lasting health.

I mistakenly thought that this man was the answer to my plight. At long last, I had found my guru. He would hold all the answers I was seeking. I was able to speak briefly with him and while he generously offered his help, the lesson from this encounter is that he, too, is affected by this mystery. But he cannot walk the road for me. He is not my guru; he is a teacher, a supporter, an affirmer of the same deep conviction. And, if nothing else, this man was instrumental on that day in March 1998 in putting me one step closer to narrowing and defining the scope of my search. Here was my first clear introduction to "Spirituality."

FROM *the* DREAM STATE:
Writing the Book

Less than a month after the seminar at Hopkins, in April of
'98, a most unusual and lengthy dream occurred:

*I am leading a group of grade school children at around
3:30 in the afternoon. We are walking in the city somewhere,
I am in the lead and as we turn a corner, I am alone. The
schoolchildren do not follow me. Intuitively I know that I cannot turn back; I feel I must continue forward. But there in the
distance are two dogs, two very distinctive dogs – bull terriers.
I believe these dogs are vicious and present a danger to me. I
break into a run and with all the strength I can muster, in one
long leap I jump and land neatly on the top of a telephone wire
that connects a telephone pole and the rooftop of what appears
to be a beach house in North Carolina. I remember expertly
balancing myself on this thick cable, which is covered with
a tarp-like material. I remember thinking that I will not get
electrocuted because the cable is wrapped in this non-conduc-
tive material.*

Steadfastly, I inch across the wire and land on the rooftop of a beach house. I am relieved to be off the tightrope but then I am high atop a tall building and feeling very apprehensive about the height. Then a small person appears; he offers me shelter in his little box on the top of the roof. This person is very, very old, withered and ancient. He is perhaps even mummified, shriveled with age. But I do not fear him, or his kindness.

There is a small, thin, red, black and white, printed cloth that lines the floor of this box. I must crawl in at the foot of the box, despite the fact that it is opened on top. The box resembles a coffin. The next thing I know, I am lying next to this person, we are side by side – I am larger than he is; he is older than I am. I have placed my arm around him and there is a nurturing feeling I have for this person, not sexual, but nurturing. I feel very safe and content. We are lying there in his box on the rooftop, looking up at the stars when I pose this question: "Had I gotten a running start, do you think I would have been able to leap as high as I did to land on that cable?"

In my heart of hearts, I knew that there was no way I could have physically performed this superhuman feat on my own, but I asked the question anyway, because I was curious to hear what my ancient companion would say. The response I received did not come from the little man next to me. It came from out of nowhere, the space was simply filled with these words: "No, it was by the grace of God that you were able to do that!"

I woke up flushed and refreshed.

By reducing the dream to writing, I found myself in a better position to understand more of its meaning. These thoughts surfaced: I am leading; I am a leader. We are all school-age because there are still life's lessons to learn. But chronologically we are adults because school is over, symbolized by the time 3:30. However, we are all still students of life.

Because of certain experiences in my life, I have "turned the corner." I have begun to awaken. I cannot reverse my life. I cannot turn back. Sensing fear or danger from that particular breed of dogs is still unclear. I have done some preliminary research on bull terriers but have yet to grasp their symbolism. Perhaps they represent the underworld, guard dogs of the underworld. Suffice it to say, I was in a fearful state. And yet I performed what would be known as a "leap of faith," represented by my jump onto the telephone/electrical wire, a cable of communication/energy. It was non-threatening because it was covered in some type of safe material.. Despite my fear of heights, I managed my way to safety on the rooftop. My sense of vulnerability was eased by the ancient figure's offer to protect me, to help me come in out of my fear. "Crawling at the foot or base of his shelter" represented the beginning, the basis of understanding. The lining of the box quite possibly symbolized this book. It was black and white and red (read) all over.

The ancient figure represents the wisdom of the ages, encased in his tomb, nurturing, protecting, quite possibly guiding me with his presence, peering out at the universe and knowing that it was, as it was said, "by the Grace of God" that I am here.

Within a short time, two dreams occur. The first:

> *A mysterious figure deep in the background comes forward, comes towards me. As this unidentified person approaches, I see that he is wearing a long, white, monk-like, hooded robe. This person slowly steps forward holding what appears to be a huge, plump, lusciously healthy crab. It is very fat and deco-*

rated like a Faberge egg, very intricately fashioned with cream and beige icing and gold beading. It reminds me of a beautiful wedding cake, yet in the shape of a crab. Very, very lovely. This crab-like creation is slowly brought over to me and is placed on my left hand, my hand is palm side down. It appears as if this crab creation will be transmitting something white to me through the vein on the top of my left hand. Once I comprehend what is happening, I immediately react, I try to pull away because I remember that there are no lymph nodes on my left side. At this point, I awake.

This dream makes me feel somewhat apprehensive and initially confused. I try different explanations – wedding cake? Wedding crab? *Wedding crab.* What's a *wedding crab*? And yet that is what is was, an ornate wedding cake in the shape of a crab. I couldn't come up with any other explanation. I just remember feeling very eerie. More occurs the next night:

I dreamt I was discussing a beach property with a rental agent. The gist of the conversation was that I wanted to rent a particular house. One that I had rented in real life the previous summer. The rental agent advised me that the property was unavailable for the week in question because the property's owners were having new carpet installed during that week. I insisted I didn't care about the inconvenience; I just wanted that house for Spring Break. But the agent stood firm.

When I awoke, I realized that the house in question was the "Happy Crab," the very house that I rented on the Outerbanks in

North Carolina. It also happened to be the same house on which I found myself on the rooftop looking at stars in the previous dream. The significance of this house is derived from my stay there the previous summer.

For the past several years, a group of women and I rent a beach house on the Outerbanks of North Carolina. We leave the husbands home, take the kids and head for the beach. One of the best things about being there is the amount of time I can spend reading. I am always looking for good reading material to take with me. Twice in one week, the book Conversations with God was recommended to me, and while I didn't have the faintest idea what it was about, I thought I should pick it up. I bought what I thought was the book and took it to the beach.

As it turned out, I mistakenly bought a workbook based on the book. It consisted of selected passages from the book and exercises designed to be used in conjunction with the book I didn't have. I tried to be open to its content and was surprised to find that I received a response to one of the exercises mentioned in the workbook. The instruction was to go to bed and make a point of remembering the first thing on your mind when you awake. I did this with some skepticism.

When I awoke, though, there was, in fact, a "message" – it was: "Examine your relationships." Just a simple little message. A message that at the time seemed a little odd. There I was at the beach, sharing a house with two girlfriends and eight kids. I didn't know what to make of it. And even now I dwell on its possible meanings. I guess in hindsight the idea was that each relationship is sacred and to be honored for whatever it brings to your life. I hadn't really made the connection before, but it does seem, in terms of timing, that the series of dreams just described – the ones about Günter, the lymphoma dream started shortly thereafter and seemed to be more frequent and intense.

I think its important to note that from the beginning these dreams were unsolicited by me. In fact, even now when I go to sleep and want badly to dream, it is really not up to me. The dreams occur when I need guidance; they do not arrive purely on my whim. I am constantly reminding myself that I don't run this ship. And this is a tiresome thing to do for the oldest of seven children who is used to having things her way.

At the time these dreams occurred, I was preoccupied with finding a beach house for Spring Break, and so I hastily chalked these back to back dreams to my subconscious desire to rent the Happy Crab again. This explanation seemed to make the most sense and so I dismissed the dreams as nothing more than that.

So, I was convinced that there was a strong reason why I should rent that beach house again. Thinking back to the previous night's dream, I interpreted it to mean nothing more than my subconscious desire to rent that particular house because it happened to be called "The Happy Crab." *Perhaps*, I thought, *I mistook this dream to be a literal interpretation of my wanting to rent this house again.* We had had such fun there the year before.

It wasn't until a few weeks later, possibly even months later, that I revisited this dream. I was in a bookstore and saw a chart that illustrated the various signs of the zodiac. What caught my eye was the zodiac sign for Cancer. It was the crab!

The dream made more sense. The wedding crab symbolized my "union," my "wedding" to the Divine through cancer. This beautiful symbol was placed on top of my left hand, the arm where the lymph nodes were removed, through which now a "white substance" flows. The white substance represents healing energy, healing light, divine white energy flowing through my veins wrought by my experience with cancer. Cancer wed me to God. That was the connection. That was the symbolism of this dream.

Curiously enough, I think it's worth noting that the second dream about the beach house was actually a precognitive one, because I did eventually rent another beach house for Spring Break that year. I settled for one very similar but a few lots closer to the beach. Why do I even mention this? Because when I went to pick up the keys for the property, the rental agent mistakenly handed me the keys to the "Happy Crab" and told me how much I would enjoy the "new carpet." Remember, now, this was something I already knew from the dream. It is a small point, but here again is a dream referencing something that would take place in the future.

It is now May 1998 and in a dream state I am having a conversation with one of my oldest and dearest friends, Debbie Skipper. During the course of the conversation, she questions me about the *writing* course I took in school. There was a strong emphasis on the word "writing" and on that note I woke up.

That was all I remember of the dream, and yet I knew it was significant because of that whole-body feeling that occurs.

Once again, I find myself awake at 5:00 a.m., lying on my back, looking up at the bedroom ceiling – this time repeating the word "writing, writing." All I can come up with is writing a book, a book about my experience. And so, laying there alone with my thoughts, I continue my one-person dialogue and ask myself, "Okay, sure, write a book about all of this and who is going to read it?" "Better yet, Anne, who is going to publish it?" And then, as if on cue, the name

Jeanne Burns rushes to my mind. Many thoughts collide with each other as the door to my mind opens.... *Write the book; the "research" will follow.*

As I listened to my inner thoughts, this directive began to take shape. I actually entertained the idea of writing a book. Once I convinced myself, writing a book seemed like a real possibility. Here was something concrete for me to undertake. I had struggled for over a year about the lymphoma research dream; the "big dream." I didn't know how to pursue such a mandate, a kindly mandate, but a mandate all the same. Initially, I tried different avenues: I contacted the local chapter of the Lymphoma and Leukemia Society; they wanted fundraisers. A neighbor referred me to a local healer, but I couldn't bring myself to leave a message on her really weird answering machine. Nothing I initiated panned out. Again, I was trying to take charge. I was trying to lead in the dance.

The suggestion to write a book felt more like a gift than a task. It was like being given the border pieces to a puzzle, defining the perimeter of my search for answers, my direction on this journey, my focus, my life's work.

Synchronicity was never more artfully displayed than three months before this dream in which writing was suggested. Frank and I had attended the grand opening of a newly expanded printing plant. As the general contractor, Frank had devoted nearly 18 months to this project, the largest he had ever undertaken.

We were invited to the opening, along with all of the customers and vendors for this printing company. The company happened to be Irish-owned, so it seemed fitting that the celebration be held on March 17th, St. Patrick's Day.

There were probably 300 people there: a mix of vendors,

clients, and employees, as well as great food, plenty to drink and authentic Irish music. Armed with my second glass of wine, I wandered off from Frank's side and headed for the food. After a few moments meandering, I spotted a woman who has just walked into the main area of the plant. I immediately recognized her as someone I knew, but couldn't for the life of me figure out how, or when. So for the better part of the night I kept her within eyeshot. At one point, I was close enough to read her nametag, "Jeanne Burns." Surely that would ring a bell. But no clue. As the evening was winding down, curiosity and wine get the best of me. I walked up to this woman and blurted out "Do we know each other?" As it turned out she too was trying to figure out how she knew me. After playing twenty questions, the mystery was solved. We had both worked at the same restaurant while in college, some 25 years ago! And yet we didn't really know each other by name. Our only contacts were brief conversations at shift change. I worked evenings and she worked days. And while we never really knew each other before, the rest of that night we had a great time laughing and carrying on.

As it turned out, Jeanne owns her own publishing company.. And to make matters more interesting, our former boss, the owner of the restaurant, had had *lymphoma* some years back and Jeanne had helped him with a macrobiotic diet. We ended the evening exchanging business cards. And if I'm not mistaken she said as we parted "Well, maybe we'll do something together one day." At it turned out her card was tossed in the bottomless pit of my purse and I didn't think any more about her; the likelihood that our paths would cross again seemed slim. That is until this book idea came about.

After the message to "write the book and the research will follow," I did in fact call Jeanne and we tried to meet, but it just wasn't in the cards at that time. I don't know whether I mentioned to her my idea of a book. I think I did and we were going to get together. But I wasn't very confident and didn't see much point in talking about a "maybe." I didn't even know what type of publisher she was. I didn't know the first thing about publishing, agents, writers, etc. The fact of the matter was, I didn't consider myself a writer. I thought perhaps there was some other way to get the dream experiences of spirit and healing across; I thought maybe I would forget about it, go on to something else, find other things that needed my attention. I thought that if I read enough books, I would eventually convince myself that what I wanted to say, had already been said, and said by a "writer." Not me.

In the back of my mind, I vacillated about writing these experiences down. Then I would get so antsy. I knew I couldn't ignore it anymore when I couldn't do the slightest menial chore without thinking, *I should be writing, I should be writing. I should be getting this off my chest. I should be releasing this from my brain. I can't do another load of clothes until I turn on that computer and get something down. I can't fix another meal, until I write this mental bantering down.*

It was my soul mate, Frank, who charged "Anne, who cares if it never gets published? You won't be free of it until you write it down. So just do it!"

Again, he was right.

This notion of writing a book was further solidified weeks later in the following dream:

I am balancing a bunch of scrambled eggs on my head. They are slipping and sliding all over the top of my head. Very messy. I am attempting to keep them on my head with a knotted scarf from the '40s. Someone, a woman, fixes this bandana-like scarf and removes several knots, flattens it and readjusts it to fit my head. I put it back on and observe the results. Then this same woman leads me to a window. Inside the window is a room; there is a bright red glow to this room, as if there is heat emanating from a hidden fireplace.

There in the center of the room is a big, hulking writing desk. Perched atop the desk is a papyrus-like shelf positioned with "y" brackets at both ends, similar to that of an ancient Indian burial stand. I see that this shelf is beginning to sag in the middle either from weight or age or both. I understand from my vantage point that I cannot sit at this desk and write until I resolve what is looming over the desk, what is looming over me. I feel a sense of urgency about this. It's as if this room will go up in flames, if I don't do something in short order.

I awake instantly to the duet of Frank and Nancy Sinatra singing, "Saying Something Stupid Like I Love You."

I lay there thinking. The scrambled eggs represent my ideas, embryonic creations in my mind. But right now they are mixed up and confused. *Scrambled.* I cannot sit at the big writing desk until I clear up old feelings that loom over me; I need a clean slate mentally before I can focus on what I want to say.

The song is very suggestive of nostalgic feelings I had for my dad. It is especially pronounced by its subject matter: "saying something stupid like "I love you" and by the fact that it is a father/daughter duet. Like other women my age, I felt a sense of longing and regret over that first heartbreak. That heartbreak was not the boy who bought me my first valentine or the handsome senior I took to the prom, but my father. One day my father stopped our love affair because I became a young woman. One day the man I admired and loved the most had to give me up, had to put distance between us. One day your father realizes that you are becoming a young woman and your relationship must change. Something is so lost and so sad, something so unspoken and so confusing.

And so as a direct result of that dream I sat down and wrote a letter to my dad expressing all the feelings I had for him, but had been unable to communicate for so many years. There was an enormous amount of therapeutic value in reducing these feelings to words, transferring them to paper.

I hesitated in sending the letter. But apparently synchronicity was at work here because that very day my brother dropped by, as did my sister, each separately. Both read the letter privately and became visibly moved. Based on their reactions, I decided it was something I needed to send, not just for me but perhaps for all of us.

My father called immediately after receiving the letter. We talked and affirmed our love for one other. It was a very moving conversation with plenty of tears. Understand, I have no expectations of changing a 75-year-old man, but I am much more at peace with our relationship, knowing that he loves me as best he can and knowing that he now knows without a doubt how much I truly love him.

Letters are wonderful things.

WHAT SPIRIT
LOOKS LIKE

The dreams are more infrequent now, despite my wish to dream every night. As I said before, it's not something I can control. I must constantly remind myself that I am not in charge. Then in June 1998 I have a very lucid dream:

> I am leaving a bookstore, trying to find my car. I can't remember where I had parked it. I am feeling ruffled because I can't find it. When I do, in fact, locate it, it is double-parked right in front of the bookstore I had just left. Feeling very frustrated with myself I said aloud, "Anne, what's with you? What is happening to you?"
>
> On that note, I turn just in time to see a tall, lanky mid-40ish man in a gray business suit get hit from behind by an automobile. He is thrown high in the air and lands back against the car with terrific force. He is battered about by the car, thrown every which way. Running towards him, I scream out for someone to call 911. By the time I reach him he is a crumbled, still mess of a person.
>
> I touch what seems to be some part of his face or head. I

can't really tell exactly where because there is a veil or a piece of fabric that covers his face. But I touch what seems to be the center of his forehead and in a soothing voice tell him that it will be "okay," that everything will be all right. At this point I don't know whether he is dead or alive.

All at once the man becomes fully animated. He leaps to his feet, catapulting himself across the very car that hit him. I watch in fascination as he becomes engrossed in an intense conversation with a woman with dark hair and fair skin (Spanish perhaps) and two small children whose ages I would put somewhere between 8 and 10.

With his back to me, I see him using his hands and gesturing in a very animated and enthusiastic manner. I can see that the children and the woman are responding to him. Their faces light up and are filled with love and understanding as they listen intently to what this man is telling them. I strain to hear their conversation but realize that it is in a language that I do not understand. They, on the other hand, show complete understanding of everything he is telling them.

I get the impression that he is reminding them of all of the times they had together, instilling in them a sense of his values and his love for them. There is a soft glow clearing emanating from this man, encasing the woman and the two children in his light.

With the same exaggerated movements, the man abruptly leaps from that position and nearly dances across the top of the auto and slumps down in a chair on the other side of the car. Now all animation ceases. I notice that in his arm is evidence of some sort of medical access.

I awake not knowing whether he is dead or alive.

I am reminded (and let me remind you as well) that at the time these dreams occur I am expecting to receive the precise message that is contained in the dream. At the time that I record the dream, certain impressions are formed and become my impression or understanding of the dream. It is only through time and life experience that I comprehend more fully the total meaning of these dreams.

So I would encourage whoever is recording their dreams to keep accurate notes and to include every detail, every feeling, every impression. Do not omit a section, merely because you do not see its merit at first blush. Write out the entire dream. Pay attention to the thoughts and feelings you have and when and how those feelings change or are enhanced during the dream. Especially remember to record your feelings at the end of the dream. I believe that many dreams are intricately woven to create a feeling in you that only culminates at the conclusion of the dream.

I am reminded again that every detail, every piece of minutia serves as a part of the whole message. Try to look at the dream as if it were a play. And in the play there is an overall theme and yet the true message of the play cannot be realized unless each act is allowed to unfold in its own time. As was the case with this most recent dream, the magnitude, depth and details of the dream were only fully realized a year later.

Having said all that, my initial impression of this lengthy dream was that it provided my first clear illustration of spirit. In one instant this man was a lifeless mass of human flesh and, in another, he was transformed by spirit, infused with life, energy, drive, attitude, passion, and love. It was as if this gangly body was nothing more than a marionette puppet that someone had rested on the ground. He was a crumpled mess of flesh only to become alive and infused with energy. For some reason I especially remember his limbs. He was extremely tall and lanky, wide in the hips. It was almost as if his "Spirit" was tangible, palpable. I could see it. And so I thought that the nature of this dream was merely to illustrate spirit or the lack thereof. The elaborateness and length of the dream led me to believe that there was probably much more to it, but I became frustrated trying to figure it out. Nothing was clicking.

For some time afterward there was a hiatus of sorts. Dreams were coming less frequently and I was losing interest. Since there were fewer dreams, there was less writing going on. I was impatient, anxious to do something. But what? In my mind there was not enough material to write a pamphlet, let alone a book.

The summer of 1998 was more than half over. The morning of August 5th I woke up repeating the phrase: "alternative medicine and complementary therapy." I was puzzled, obviously. Who wakes up chanting a phrase like that? That's what it felt like. It felt like I had said it over and over again for quite some time. It felt as if someone programmed me.

Do you pay attention to what's laying on your mind's plate first thing in the morning? What's the first thing you think about when you wake up? Do you ask, "What's the weather doing?" Or, "Do I have a meeting this morning?" "Is today trash day?" Mine is: "Can I sleep another five minutes?"

So it did strike me a little odd that I was mouthing this popular phrase, a phrase that has become commonplace marketing jargon by today's health care providers, advertised to consumers that they will receive more that just routine medical care.

Perhaps it was surfacing because of the seminar I had attended back in March at Johns Hopkins. These were popular buzz words bantered about non-stop during the entire two-day seminar.

But that wasn't it; there was something else about this phrase that really bugged me. Repeating it over and over, I realized what troubled me. It wasn't the phrase itself; it was the manner in which I was saying it. I was changing the emphasis on the syllables. I was saying **alter**-native medicine and **complement**-tree therapy. By separating the syllables and changing the accent, these words were now parsed out and used as verbs to suggest something entirely different.

Alter by definition means to "change, reverse, stop" and **complement** means to complete, supplement, balance, harmonize. And so now the phrase meant something entirely different – stop, change, reverse native medicine, and I guess in my case that would be conventional medicine. Complete or supplement-tree therapy. Could this be referring to Taxol (a cancer drug extracted from the bark of a tree)? Or could "tree" therapy mean just that: connecting with nature again – trees.

There may be nothing to this. Years ago, I would have dismissed these thoughts, but I am no longer a novice to the power of dreams. I am reminded of that fateful early afternoon nap. I awoke and there it stood waiting patiently at the gate of my mind, waiting for me to awake, waiting for me to acknowledge the simple statement that there was *"something lodged under your arm."*

That little suggestion saved my life. Because the fact of the matter is that the mass in my lymph nodes had shown up on mammograms in 1990 and 1991. But no mention was made because "enlarged lymph nodes are seen all the time." No medical doctor had picked up on the fact that I had cancer in my lymph nodes despite my annual mammograms.

And so this is evidently some sort of directive. As of this writing, I haven't any further clues on the matter unless to suggest that we ease off the chemicals and balance or harmonize the treatment of cancer patients by caring for their spirits, engaging them at a "soul" level. Right now that remains to be seen.

♦ ♦ ♦

Two dreams occur again, back to back. The first:

Frank and I are both reading separately a passage about the stigmata, possibly about Padre Pio. Then we realize the synchronicity of both of us reading about the same subject at the same time.

My interpretation was short and sweet. Frank and I are kindred spirits and we both basically believe the same truths, as if to say we were both on the "same page" in a spiritual sense.

The dream that followed was more elaborate and revealing:

Frank and I are in a large arena, possibly a stadium, then it changes to a big beach house with my whole family there. At this point Frank is holding a very small infant and attempting to feed it quite unsuccessfully with a white, plastic, toy bottle. The child is trying desperately to feed, but can't because it is a fake bottle.

I grab the baby from Frank, realizing instantly that this infant is very hungry and hasn't been properly nourished. I

*can see from the baby's face that it has the ability to be fat and
healthy by the size of its cheeks. But at the moment its cheeks
are flat and flabby, nothing more than thin layers of skin lying
on either side of its face, like flattened saddle bags.*

*I realize that this child is starving and that only I can save
it, that I am the one who knows how to feed it and make it
grow full and healthy.*

This is a fairly easy one to interpret. Back when I quit my job,
I truly thought that my time would be best spent taking care of my
kids and helping my husband with his construction business. And
while all of this was easily accomplished, there were still restless feelings, pervading notions that there was something more I needed to
do. As much as I wanted to share Frank's enthusiasm about building,
I knew in my heart of hearts this was his passion, not mine. And so
this dream further solidified my need to feed my own creativity, my
own "baby." No one else can do this for me. I am the only one who
recognizes its potential; I am the only one who knows how best to
nourish my "baby," how to make it grow and thrive.

It's now September 1998. The dreams have all but ceased. I still
question my direction at least once a day; it's like my engine is on
but in neutral. Spinning my wheels at this point, I content myself
with keeping house, getting the kids back to school and working
more with Frank. I try to keep things in perspective and relax a little
bit. More or less put my life on automatic pilot.

September happens to be my birth month and also serves as my
health maintenance month. The usual favorites are scheduled: GYN
exam, Mammogram, Blood Tests, Chest X-Ray, Overall Physical
and Cancer Checkup. In prior years my gyn doctor was a foreigner,

usually Asian, who spent about two minutes examining me and even less time talking in short blips of broken English.

But this year it's different. When my appointment is made, the secretary decided to give me someone new. I told her it didn't matter to me; I just wanted the next available appointment with whomever. So, expecting another brief gyn encounter, I'm sitting in the examining room in my paper gown and in walks a very charming, handsome, likable guy about my age. He spent a good deal of time reviewing my medical file, a binder that now looks like a draft of *War and Peace*. He finishes most of the routine checkup questions; checks the file again, looks up at me and says "How was the lump discovered?" When I told him that I had found it, he seemed somewhat taken aback because it was in such an out of the way spot. As a matter of fact, I remember how difficult it was to locate for the surgeon. How I had to first find it myself and then lead his hand to the exact spot. It really was buried deep in the cavity of my armpit.

At this point he closed my massive medical file, looked me straight in the eyes and said "Well, young lady, you should have been dead by now. God must have other plans for you."

Well, you could have knocked me over. I know his intention was to be upbeat and positive, but his remarks just shocked me. Especially bringing God into the equation. In all my years I have never known any doctor to mention God in conversation unless of course it's in some reference to his/herself (only kidding). After regaining my composure I felt that perhaps this whole exercise, my entire visit, was merely one of many roadside reminders that I did, in fact, have a mission of some sort.

HOPE'S MESSAGE

In the early fall of 1998, Frank stopped by the office mid-morning to take care of some paperwork. He tells me a friend's son, a young man in his early 20s, was recently diagnosed with lymphoma. For some reason, learning of this makes me very upset. I didn't know him personally, but I knew his father. After Frank left, I started to cry uncontrollably; it's as if I needed to do something for this guy. I needed to tell him something – and so I wrote.

Dear Friend,
I have heard that you have cancer.
I know how frightened and terribly isolated
you feel right now.
I know that this event in your life could not
have been more unexpected,
Could not have happened at a more inappropriate time.
That is why I am writing to you.
I want to tell you that it will be all right,
That your spirit can get you through this,
That at some point in time you will be truly joyous.
This burden you now carry was given to you by God.

Because cancer will change your life.

Cancer is a gift.

A perfect gift from God.

An awakening to what is truly important in your life.

It's as if you have gone around this world

for a long time not really awake,

Not really living.

Yes, you have struggled, you have sacrificed,

You have worked hard, you have had faith,

You have believed in yourself,

You have hated, you have loved, you have forgiven,

But for what? For what have you done all of this?

Do you know?

Do you know your Self?

Do you know that God lives in you and you in Him?

If you really knew this all along then perhaps

you wouldn't be sick right now.

I don't want you to feel guilty, because

there is nothing to feel guilty about.

You were unaware.

We all are (were) unaware.

I was unaware.

Even worse, I thought I was aware

And all the while I really wasn't.

It has been nearly seven years and

I can still remember it all so vividly

That's why it is easy for me to know what you are experiencing.

And yet, I am here today for a reason.

I have been told in no uncertain terms that I really do have a purpose.

My reason for being is to bring you comfort,
To let you know that it truly will be all right.
I want to be a source of peace for you,
And while I would want more than anything else
to do this in person,
My emotions prevent me from being as effective
as hopefully this letter will be.
Surrender is the operative word here.
You can pray,
You can panic,
You can plead,
You can place your life in the hands of the doctor.
But what is really needed is surrender,
Total, unconditional surrender to the love of God.
To his peace, his will.
Hopefully you will reach, if you have not already,
a point of absolute terror.
And the terror is not the cancer,
or the battery of tests that you will undergo,
Or the look in the doctor's eyes,
or the sound of his voice,
Or the results on a piece of paper;
The terror comes from realizing for the first time
in all the years you have been here
That you are not in control.
Your life is under the direction of another.
The another is God.
And when you finally come to this realization,
When you finish negotiating out all the things

you promise to do if you live,
All the emotional baggage you vow to release,
How you will now finally smell the coffee,
The roses, your child's hair, the fall leaves,
When all of this still doesn't bring your release
from the grip of pure terror,
When this happens,
When you cannot worry one more minute
whether you will live or die,
When you think you cannot stand to wake up another morning and
realize that this nightmare is real
and you are living it,
When you cannot swallow this truth one more minute,
Something will happen...
You will surrender.
You will surrender your will.
You will realize that it's all right to die.
It's just living that you will miss.
There will come a point when you realize
that everyone takes the high dive,
Some before others.
And when you reach that point,
When you really do,
A peace will come over you and it will be all right.
The panic will end
And you will have met that which has
caused you so much fear
And you will know it as love.
God's love for you.

Because now you will have remembered
what you and I and everyone else had forgotten:
that God's love is all there is.
In the grand scheme of things
(And it really is a scheme),
There is only God, the Beginning and the End.
And with that realization it's okay.
And by this I don't mean you should despair.
I don't mean in anger submit to his Will
because you have no other choice.
Because there is no anger in this place
I am talking about.
You are not angry anymore.
You are part of a larger force and that Force
is guiding you,
Through whatever is in store for you.
And you are all right.
You will work with your doctors,
You will give love and receive love,
You will not be angry and you
will show others the way,
As I am showing you.
And whatever the outcome, you will be at peace.
Because this gift of cancer is your
connection to the Divine.
For people like you and I perhaps there is
no other way to show us the Way.
And so dear Friend there is nothing more
I need tell you.

Bless this event and use it to become
the Godlike person that you are.
Someday we will meet
In the meantime you will use this letter to help another,
Because by doing so you help yourself.
You will help awaken God in others.

I can't honestly say where parts of this came from. I cried through most of it, and cried every time I reread it. Then I guess at some point I put it down and felt that perhaps some day, some one may find it helpful.

Here was my first desperate attempt to reach out and help someone who had just been diagnosed. I wanted to say these things, to make it all right, to bring some semblance of calm to the terror. To this day I cannot read this letter without some tears. I suppose I relive those moments: the shock, the surrender, the peace, the love, the Gift. I am truly grateful for all that has happened to me. I am also convinced that I cannot specifically direct peace, I can only put it out there and hope that it reaches those who need it.

✦ ✦ ✦

The Christmas holidays are upon us and I find myself sitting across from Sister Theresa Mary, my youngest daughter's former teacher, having our annual holiday dinner at a local restaurant. Over the past few years I had developed a nice relationship, a genuine friendship, with Sr. Theresa Mary. At least twice a year, usually after the close of school and then again around the holidays, we go out to eat. I remember this particular holiday dinner I was voicing instantly that was the very reason I was asked to watch Oprah.

Still unsure as to what my role in this would be, I eventually got his name and address, through Sr. Theresa Mary, who knew someone at the Mayo Clinic. After nearly two weeks of vacillating about what to do, I sent a letter to Walter Peyton explaining exactly what had happened to me and the reason for my letter. No reply. I am sure he was inundated with well-wishers after that spot on Oprah, but the lack of response only deepened my frustration about the whole matter. I felt like I just wasn't being effective and, yet, clearly I was being directed to do something with "hope." Hope was the common ingredient in both instances: the Wilkerson woman with alepecia and Walter Peyton's rare liver cancer. But how was I to effect any change?

I still marvel at the fact that there was a voice that morning who told me to "watch Oprah today." And what's even more astonishing was my reaction to that voice, or I guess I should say my "non-reaction." I mean, why didn't I just freak out? I'd never had anything like that happen before. Dreams, yes, strong mental suggestions, yes, symbolic songs, yes, but never, never a voice outside of myself. I fail to comprehend why I am not crazy over this fact. Honestly, inject me with a huge dose of sodium phenothol and I would still say that's what happened, because that is what happened; and yet I have no plausible explanation for this or any of the other events, which are the subject of this book. You can imagine why at times I think that this is a total waste of energy because no one is going to believe me. Even I have trouble with this one. I mean, Jung had dreams; precognitive and otherwise, and Freud interpreted dreams, but did they hear a voice? I mean a regular voice. I just don't know. And yet I do now. I know what happened. I am not now, nor was I then, afraid

my trepidation over what I should do if I were to talk with people about my experience. What would I say without sounding crazy? She answered unhesitatingly, "Oh, Anne, God will tell you what to say." Now why didn't I think of that? Her answer was so simple and straightforward.

During dinner, Sister and I spent a great deal of time talking about John, the husband of one of the teachers at school. John was 42 years old and had two children that also attended the school. He had been diagnosed with esophageal cancer and was facing an uncertain outcome. It occurred to me during our conversation that perhaps he would benefit from the "Dear Friend" letter. I asked that Sr. Theresa Mary read it, and if she considered it appropriate to pass it on to him anonymously. Which is exactly what she did.

In early February 1999, I wake up saying "Wilkerson's Disease." And then I recall a lengthy dream, the gist of which is all I remember. There was an entire family that had given up hope. They had all resigned themselves; all the members of the family were gravely ill. As an observer in this dream, I became very upset over the fact that they were all so hopeless. I asked one of them the name of the disease and he answered "Wilkerson's Disease." And so I awoke saying, "Wilkerson's Disease."

I had never heard of such a malady. Did I misunderstand? Maybe it was "Parkinson's Disease." But I kept repeating "Wilkerson's Disease." Then I started playing with the phrase and came up with "will cure son's disease." Now that got me pretty excited because my son has Cystic Fibrosis and I thought that perhaps there was some connection there. But there were no further thoughts, no clues.

The following day, my nurse friend, Salli, stopped by for coffee. She had never heard of Wilkerson's Disease, but according to her, they are naming new diseases all the time. She promised to look into it for me.

For some reason she also had occasion to stop by the very next day, this time accompanied by her daughter, Ashley. Ashley was in her first year of high school and, for some inexplicable reason, I asked the name of her gym teacher. She casually replied,"Oh, gee, that's Mrs. Wilkerson. She's real sick. She's lost all her hair; I think she has cancer." Salli and I shot each other a look of disbelief. What a coincidence!

I felt compelled to contact Mrs. Wilkerson and offer whatever help I could. As it turned out, she did not have cancer; but she was still extremely open to my call. She was fascinated that I had just dreamt of someone named Wilkerson. She explained that she had been in a very bad marriage for several years and, as a direct result, now suffered with a condition called "alepecia" which in severe cases, like hers, causes complete irreversible baldness. This explained why her students thought she had cancer. As soon as she told me she had alepecia, I relayed the story of Frank's bout with the same condition earlier in his life and how he now, years later, sports a full head of hair. This woman was so happy to hear that because she said she had "given up hope." None of her doctors had offered any encouragement at all. She was thankful that we had an opportunity to talk, and that I offered some form of hope.

A similar incident occurred two mornings later. This was not a dream but an actual event:

It's early morning, Frank has just left for work and I am lying there on my side assessing how many more minutes of sleep I can steal before getting the kids up and ready for school,

when I hear a perfectly clear voice say to me: "Watch O today." This voice was neither male nor female. It wasn't or soft, it was just a perfectly calm, level voice out of now It was as if someone was invisibly standing right by me. I emphasize that this was not a dream. I was lying there awake!

With a start I sat up in bed and looked around. The one there. Everyone was still asleep, even the dog that lay a And yet I heard a voice. A voice telling me to watch Opra

I shook my head in disbelief saying "okay, sure, wat today." On that thought, I got out of bed and set into m own version of a Chinese fire drill to get four kids to time.

The rest of my day went off without a hitch. I actually morning directive. It just slipped out of my mind as so m do when you are orchestrating four little lives as well as It's now late afternoon and I am busy making dinner whe Frankie spills the entire contents of his binder on the land clubroom. Homework, test papers, and announcements al everywhere. I help him gather his junk at the same time daughter, Kaitlyn, is turning on "Oprah." It's four o'clock! ately remembered the morning missive and sank to the bo curious to see what Oprah had in store for her viewers tha

But, before Oprah began her scheduled show, sh in to the Mayo Clinic by satellite, to wish her good frien Payton, well. He was being treated for a rare form of li She implored the audience to pray for him and give him soon as I heard this I experienced that total energy rush

of this voice. So who was it? A ghost, a spirit guide, the Divine, an angel. I haven't the faintest idea. I only know what I know. And I know there was a voice the morning of February 5, 1999 telling me to watch Oprah.

SPIRIT DREAM
REVISITED

In June, 1999, John, the teacher's spouse with esophageal cancer, passed away. Because he and his wife were so well-known and liked in our school community there was a tremendous outpouring of support. I was enlisted to help at the wake after his funeral. Everyone brought food and beverages. After awhile I took a few moments to walk through the rectory garden and discovered that John's wife had made a display, a collage of photos of their life together. There were early college pictures, pictures of their wedding, their children, friends, and relatives, all lovingly arranged. As if by chance one photo stood out; one single shot caught my eye. It had this vague feeling of familiarity. It was a picture of John standing and I immediately recognized not his face, but his physique. It was that of the unidentifiable person in the dream I had exactly one year ago, the lengthy dream about the tall, lanky mid-40ish businessman who was hit by a car. The dream in which I receive a clear picture of what "spirit" looks like.

As soon as I got home, I reread the dream about "spirit" and this time all the pieces fell into place. John was the figure in my dream about "spirit." John was the man in the suit who was struck from behind, not by a car, but by cancer! When you are told you have cancer, it feels exactly like getting hit by a car. Cancer catches you totally unaware; it hits you from behind, throwing you high in the air, beating you about.

In the dream, I touch his forehead, but John's face is veiled; my connection to John was made through the letter. I touched some part of John's mind through the anonymous letter sent at Christmastime via Sr. Theresa Mary.

It was all so clear now. In the dream John is communicating on a level I cannot understand, a language that I do not know. In the dream its a foreign language. That language is the language of love he has for his wife and his two children. John's wife Joan is fair-skinned with black hair, easily mistaken for a Latin or Spanish woman. John left behind two boys close in age to the children in the dream. He eventually died in hospice care which explains why, in the dream, there is an IV or medical access in his arm. And though John died, I have to believe from the dream that he was healed before his death and that much healing occurred within his family.

And perhaps most important of all, I have to believe John died at peace.

As of this writing, I have not told his wife any of this, for many reasons, not the least of which is that I have finally learned that, despite all my enthusiasm about the mystical side of life, others do not necessarily share that enthusiasm or are, for whatever reason, not at this juncture in their life prepared to venture off the tried and true path into side streets of mysticism or spiritual adventure.

It's as if you head for the beach, your paradise, but you always take the interstate every time you go. You never venture down a country road, or a rambling hillside, and, as such, miss so much of the beauty, richness and opportunity of the journey. And so after a year or two of talking about this other fascinating part of life, I realize that many would rather just take the interstate. However polite or interested they may act, the fact of the matter is, at this juncture in their travels there is no interest in exploring the layers of their existence, finally understanding that the seemingly chance happenings of life are, in reality (real reality) the total tapestry of living a life fully aware and conscious. Only during those deliberate moments when we elect to detach from our selves and the routineness of our life, can we savor and delight in the pure viewing pleasure at the unveiling of synchronicities in our lives.

LIFE GUIDANCE FROM
the DREAM STATE

During the Summer of 1999, my practice was to read at random passages from *A Course in Miracles* every morning as part of my daily meditation. The idea that "you only get what you give" was repeatedly reinforced. I suppose this book is my way of giving, because it seems to be the only way to release myself from the feeling that I am not doing enough to promote lessons of spirituality among people dealing with cancer. And yet how can I convince someone else that what helped me can help them? Maybe my task is not to worry about convincing but merely to get the word out and then let them take from it what rings true. Maybe I shouldn't be so concerned about what works for me.

One thing is certain – I am hooked on dreams. I'm talking incessantly about them. I've developed a minor reputation among family and friends as the dream master. Interpreting dreams seemed to come easily to me. I helped a younger sister work with her dreams to determine how she should handle a problem marriage. I still record my own dreams, most of which deal with family issues and personal growth; they serve as illustrative examples of what is occurring in my waking state and how I should perceive these events. These dreams ranged from how to reach a deeper level of understanding of my teenage daughter to recognizing areas of my marriage that need attention.

In August, I got into a heated argument with my better half about not taking this book seriously, about how, in his mind, I am someone who lacks perspective, who has no concept of introspection. Of course I countered that this was pure bunk. This minor disagreement precipitated a discussion about our first daughter, Kate. You see, at age 13 and 46 we were at odds with each other.

On August 21, 1999, around the time of our argument, this dream occurred:

I was sitting in the first car I ever owned, a 1969 Datsun 2000, a fast little yellow convertible. I was in a parking lot positioned at a stop sign ready to take off. I had test driven the car around the parking lot; it was running great (something it did infrequently in real life; it was yellow because it was a "lemon"). Through my rear-view mirror I saw my daughter Kate was having a difficult time; she was trying to get out of a parking space and needed my help. I went back to take her place behind the wheel and noticed that her car was a brown, nine-passenger '64 Chevy wagon, the same one my family had when I was her age. The back of the wagon was full of stuff, and I had to get out and pack everything back in the car and shut the back door before the car could move.

The vehicles in this dream are very important. The first represents my own persona; how I perceive myself. In my mind's eye I am still 19 years old, fast and cute, ready to take off, ready to leave my parked position in life and travel the roads. However, the dream suggests that I take a look behind me. I need to understand that my daughter Kate is at the same place I was when our family owned that 1964 Chevy wagon. I need to go back and recall the feelings of a young girl, the meaningless baggage she carries and how very often we get stuck in a space that doesn't allow us the freedom to move through our life effortlessly, without fear. I perhaps needed to help pick up all the stuff she feels is important to carry at her age and assist her in getting unstuck, getting her act on the road.

A LESSON *in* PERCEPTION

Around this same time a close friend of mine, Cara, told me of her reoccurring dream in which she climbs a high tower with her two children in tow. She reaches the top of the tower and a tremendous tidal wave crashes down over her. Right before this happens she turns to her children and tells them she loves them and then says goodbye. She hates this dream and is very puzzled by it. I try to help her, offer different ideas, books to read, etc., but it has me stumped as well.

Then one night I have a similar dream:

> *I am on the beach among family and friends sitting high on the beach, in the dunes, far away from the surf. Suddenly, out of nowhere, a huge wave comes crashing down. I am submerged and then burst through jumping up and down excitedly. Then, without a moment's notice, another wave comes crashing over me. Again I just submerge and burst through, each time feeling completely exhilarated and rejuvenated.*

The dream provides insight about Cara's reoccurring dream. In both hers and mine, waves are crashing down over us. She is alone, isolated in a tower. I think it's important to note that Cara happens to be very wealthy and lives in a grand home in a very exclusive area. Perhaps this tower she has climbed so alone is the tower of material wealth. In any event, we both experience the crashing of waves over us. The wave of water represents change. I look at change as fun and exhilarating. Cara, on the other hand, perceives change as fear, or the end of her life, a real sense of dread. Here you have very similar scenarios; the key lies in one's perception. It is one's perceptions that make this dream either enjoyable or fearful.

A NEW DIRECTION

September rolls around! The children are back in school and I am looking forward to Fall, probably my favorite season, when this elaborate and illustrative dream occurred:

I am in a room with many open, receptive people and I am having a great time talking with all of them. It seems very natural and easy for me. I am on, entertaining the crowd, so to speak. The ability to truly communicate is a wonderfully satisfying feeling. But out of the corner of my eye I spot one man in the side of the room who is angry. Initially I think he is angry with me, maybe not with me personally, but with what I represent. I look over at him but he abruptly turns away in a childlike manner.

At some point, I am getting ready to leave and again glance over in his direction. He is still in a somewhat dark, but maybe less recalcitrant state, more like a pouting child. I sense there is an ever-so-slight chance, a small window of opportunity to approach him, his wall of defense seeming to have dropped ever so slightly.

I hesitate to approach, but it's as if I am being lead to do this. I'd

much prefer to stay with all the folks that are so open and receptive to
me. But, as in other dreams I've had, there is a presence, as if someone
is standing by me or behind me. At this person's insistence, I reluctantly.
approach the angry man I force myself to extend my hand, to trust that
this is the right thing to do. Facing him, I take hold of his left hand with
my left hand and then gently place my right hand over top of his.

He is sitting at a school desk with one side open. There is a clock
on the desk. As I am holding his hand I am also anxiously trying to
look at the clock. I ask the person who seems to be standing behind
me, "How long is this going to take?" And at that moment, the clock
is violently thrown face down on the desk, a desk that is now shaking
uncontrollably because a powerful surge of energy has shot through my
body from behind my right shoulder, traveled down my left arm and
into this man!

It happened so quickly and with such intensity that I was forced awake,
momentarily stunned, unable to remember who, what or where I am. It was
as if, for that moment, I was not a person, I was not a human being; I was
merely an object, an instrument, a conduit for some phenomenal force.

At this exact point these words echoed in my mind: "Lord, make me
an instrument of your peace." I am excited and frightened at the same time.
Because I was thrown awake so vehemently, I never saw the man's reaction to
what had occurred.

My left arm was wrapped around Frank's shoulder; my cheek was
pressed tightly against his back. I was slumped down below his shoulders, as
if I was hiding from my dream. I was waiting to breathe. When I did breathe
at last, I had trouble leveling my emotions.

There was a very visceral feeling to this dream. Again it was a
"totally unique experience," one that renders words meaningless. It
was as if I was deadened to physical, bodily feeling but electrified to

an outer source. I felt as if I were detached from the whole sensation, yet feeling it at the same time, being able to experience it and observe it simultaneously. I was watching and feeling myself as a channel, a conduit, an instrument to something much larger than anything I could ever conjured in my wildest imaginings, a higher power of some sort.

The dream shocked me. The ending was so unexpected. I was led over to someone I did not want to approach, I was asked to do something I wasn't comfortable doing, taking his hand, making an effort. I felt very awkward and wanted to get out of situation. And then, without warning, I was removed from my Self long enough to experience a phenomenal display of power and magnificence. There was nothing I actually did of my own accord other than take an angry man's hand. I felt as if I was merely the means to an end, an end I never saw because I woke up.

I think there are two ways to interpret this dream. One would be a fairly rational, logical one. This dream simply means that I should literally "reach out" in the absolute sense of the word and get in touch with cancer patients. I say cancer patients because I got the sense from the dream that that is with whom I was communicating. The vague surroundings in the dream were reminiscent of the outpatient center at St. Agnes Hospital where I was treated. The desk in the dream is similar to the type of chair that is used to administer the chemotherapy; the side panels fold to an upright position similar to a school desk.

The maybe not so rational, wilder, gut sense of this dream is that I will at some juncture be used in a healing capacity. In my heart of hearts this is the real explanation for such a powerful experience.

VOLUNTEERING

Within a week of this major dream event, I contacted St. Agnes Hospital and practically begged to volunteer in the outpatient oncology department. Based upon the impressions left by the dream it seemed evident that I needed to do something more than sit around and vacillate about whether this book would ever happen, would ever be of any benefit.

So, as of October 1999, I have been working with cancer patients in the very same cancer center that so lovingly treated me eight years ago. Actually, working isn't the word – the word is giving and receiving. Giving of myself and receiving tenfold in love, humor, compassion, understanding, gratitude and so much more. Every Thursday and sometimes other days of the week, I am truly being my authentic spirit. As Gary Zukov so aptly describes in *Seat of the Soul*, I have aligned my personality with the work of my soul.

Picture a sometimes blonde, currently redheaded, 47-year old woman on the brink of the second half of her life, happily jogging down the hall to deliver stat blood, or pushing the lunch cart and helping patients fantasize that tuna is really Maryland lump crab meat and ham and cheese is really filet mignon. More importantly, though, patients and I are sharing directly – one on one or sometimes in small intimate groups – our experiences, commonalities, humanness, hopes and fears. Those that wish share their dreams and we try to figure out what they mean, try to understand the reason for their cancer, or in many cases, its reoccurrence.

One of my first encounters was with a lovely woman in her mid 60s being treated for a reoccurrence of breast cancer. She and I talked at length. She was a very spiritual person, whose demeanor was calm and accepting. She expressed a strong belief in God and stated that if "God wanted [her], [she] was all right with that." She beamed with pride as she told me about her two successful children and all their wonderful accomplishments. She also told me of a son that had died of leukemia when he was ten.

Later that evening, on my way home, I thought about why such a peaceful, loving, accepting woman would again be visited by cancer and it occurred to me that perhaps this woman was still mourning the death of her 10-year-old son. And since the breast is close to the heart, that perhaps this is how her grief continues to manifest itself.

To further buttress this notion, there was another woman being treated for ovarian cancer, whom I met the following week. It had reoccurred some three years after her original incident. She was a spry late-60ish woman who seemed very involved in life, very active, and dressed attractively. Yet here she was being treated again. Through our conversations I learned that she had two grown children, a boy and a girl and that her son was going through a very difficult divorce. Then, as if it were something she needed to add, she told me that both of her children were adopted. Again, could this be a clue to the ovarian issue? Perhaps this woman perceived a sense of inadequacy in the childbearing department, or has unresolved issues in that area?

At that time, I made myself a mental note to start recording any and all impressions I receive about patients from our brief meetings – both what is said and unsaid.

PATIENT STORIES

JAN

I hadn't been volunteering too long when a patient, Mr. Clark, abruptly burst into the treatment area and announced his goodbyes to the nursing staff and the general oncology outpatient population. Evidently he had received the untimely news from his treating physician that he had only six months to live. He said he was glad his doctor had leveled with him. He planned to move to Las Vegas as soon as possible.

I could tell the nurses were visibly moved. I felt that seldom, if ever, do they receive this type of closure, this type of finality to all that they do. I would suspect that if someone is not improving then eventually they make their way to the hospital ward and then probably on to some form of hospice care.

In any event, after a tearful goodbye, Mr. Clark left and the nurses turned their attention to the ramifications this devastating news would have on his close cancer buddy, Jan. Jan, married with two young children was, at the tender age of 29, being treated for advanced lung cancer.

I had heard the nurses speak of Jan in recent weeks. They were circulating a suggested list of Christmas gifts for Jan's family, in particular her children. The nurses told me she was terminal and in all likelihood would not live to see Thanksgiving, much less Christmas. Hearing of Mr. Clark's unfortunate news, the nurses worried, might hasten Jan's departure.

The following week, I overhead a conversation between two of the nurses. Evidently Mr. Clark had phoned one of the nurses at home and told her that he had spoken with God and asked that God take him and spare Jan. The nurse thought he must have been really out of it to say something so bizarre. I, on the other hand, did not think it so bizarre.

Two days before Thanksgiving, I was working in tandem with Betty, another volunteer. Betty has been following Jan's situation from the beginning. She was very emotionally involved with Jan and her family. Betty stated that Jan was brought into the hospital over the weekend and was now on life support. It was doubtful whether she would live to Thanksgiving. To hear this was very sad.

I was somewhat intrigued by Jan and the effect she has had on the whole department. At some juncture, Betty and I took another patient, being admitted for dehydration, up to the seventh floor of the hospital, in-patient oncology. Since it was my first time up in the inpatient area, I was in unfamiliar territory, so Betty led the way and I commandeered the wheelchair. I wondered if we would get a chance to see Jan, and I asked Betty if we could visit her. Betty stated rather protectively that Jan was on the second floor and that she had plans to go in to see her before she left for the day. In words unspoken Betty let me know that Jan was her charge and to "butt out." I understood her feelings. After all, I am a total stranger. Anyway, I still wish I had had the opportunity to see Jan so that I could have put a face to the name that was in everyone's constant thoughts in outpatient oncology.

The winter months were approaching when I learned through one of the nurses that a new position was opening up in the department. They needed someone who would assist the nurses with scheduling, inputting information into the computer, filing, etc. They encouraged me to apply. I was hesitant; it didn't sound like it was what I was looking for, but I vowed to go home and sleep on the idea. Try to remain open.

And so that night I went to sleep and spent most of the night, or so it felt, working with Jan, someone whom I never had the chance to meet.

I feel the distinct sensation that I have flown in to see Jan at the hospital. I am in her hospital room, by her side. I cannot see her face, only her eyes. The very first thing I tell her is that she should not worry about her children; they will be fine. I can see them in the distance.

The next thing I remember doing is taking hold of her hand. I see my left arm next to hers in the bed. We are holding hands and yet they appear now to be gossamer, near iridescent white, as if, in the light, they have merged. I ask, "Jan, do you think that maybe your Mind can heal you?" all the while wondering What in the world am I saying to her? What has possessed me to say something like that? *And while I don't remember any more of what I said I do remember looking into her eyes and they were very distant, as if they were in a long, long tunnel, very small, very far away and yet, as we worked together, they came closer to me, closer to the surface, closer to the present.*

At some point I felt as if she was going to be all right. Then outside of her room, or beyond where we were I saw a small boy. It could have been my son, Frankie, or some child that looked like him. He was skipping ahead, lighthearted, frolicking, and it was as if he was leaving stones, or small landmarks behind, for us to follow, showing us the path to take.

I awoke in a unique manner. The time was just before dawn, and I felt as if someone had gently rolled me over onto my back, which caused me to awake very softly and slowly. Intuitively I felt that Jan was better, improved, perhaps even on her way to healing. I was very peaceful, very positive, laying there staring up at the ceiling. But at the same time I felt exhausted. I felt as if I had been working all night long, as if I really had traveled to her bedside and talked and worked through the night to bring her back.

Initially I thought this dream was responding to my indecision about pursuing the clerical opening in oncology. The dream's message was that my place is at a patient's bedside, not in front of a computer.

At my next volunteer day, I waited for a propitious moment to ask the charge nurse what had happened to Jan. They had all expected her to die before Thanksgiving. She remarked off-handedly, "Would you believe Jan went home? She came off life support and they let her go home. That girl has some will!" I was ecstatic. Still, I wanted desperately to find out more of the details, but I also knew that my inordinate curiosity about Jan and her condition might somehow draw unwanted attention to me. And so I temporarily contented myself with this bit of information. Perhaps someday, I thought, we would meet and I could get answers to my questions. Did she dream that night? What did she remember? After Christmas, I asked for the update on Jan. "She died," said one of the nurses. But evidently before she passed she had requested that everyone come to her funeral dressed in jeans; she wanted it to be very casual and lighthearted.

So what do I make of the fact that Jan made some type of remarkable recovery, albeit short lived, from her near death condition? She left the hospital, went home for a few weeks and then died at Christmas. Was there any connection to my nocturnal experience and her return home? Did any true "healing" occur during that brief interim?

Somehow I can't rule out the possibility that perhaps there was some significance to all of this prior to her death. But then again, if I am to know it will manifest itself at the appropriate time. I must constantly remind myself to have no expectations but to give openly, not based on whatever obsessive interests may satisfy my ego.

ℬONNIE

I continue to volunteer at St. Agnes, usually every Thursday, sometime twice a week if they need me. Actually, I'd be there every day if I could. I need this connection. I need to be there. It is the wellspring of my energy; it is where every good thing about my being emanates. It is where I feel my true spirit at work.

I do my best to stay open and available to talk with patients about anything they want to talk about. Every opportunity for patients and I to exchange benefits both of us.

After a couple of months under my belt as a volunteer, I invariably end up asking patients if they dream. And surprisingly, many of them do.

One patient in particular comes to mind. Her name is Bonnie. She is a petite, attractive woman in her mid-50s with strikingly beautiful blue eyes and soft white/gray hair, slightly wavy. She is being treated for a reoccurrence of breast cancer that had originally surfaced 14 years prior. We talked a bit about why it had come back. There was virtually no stress in her life; she and her husband were happily married and seemed quite devoted to each other. He was always there with her during treatment. By both of their admissions, their lives were content, their children grown and leading happy lives of their own. They had no worries – monetary or otherwise. They were just beginning to enjoy their second half of life. So we wondered why this had happened? I was dumbstruck. I couldn't even think of any questions to ask without appearing too probing. After all, I was just the volunteer there to offer them lunch.

Yet the three of us decided that we would spend some time trying to figure it out. And while I wanted to sit down and spend more time with this nice couple, I knew our initial meeting had run its course. That is, until I asked one question – my favorite. "Are you dreaming?" And with that, Bonnie turned to her husband and immediately recalled the dream that she had had just the night before. She was restless and couldn't get to sleep because she was anxious about the results of some fluid her doctor had removed from her stomach. When sleep finally did come, she fell into a dream and recounted the following:

I am standing by a lake watching a very graceful, beautiful ice skater. She is skating all over the lake. I watch and worry because I see big cracks in the ice and large bumps. I am fearful

that she will lose her balance and fall between the cracks. I am
very anxious for her. And yet to my amazement and despite all
the obstacles on the lake and huge cracks in the ice, the skater
never faltered, or broke stride, but continued moving effortlessly
without interruption across the lake, full of grace and confi-
dence.

Bonnie had no idea what this dream meant, and actually had
no intention of even trying to figure it out. Had I not asked, it
would have in all probability faded into her memory.

I blurted out my strong initial impression of the dream. In my
mind, this dream was undoubtedly a very real, tangible message of
hope. Part of Bonnie, the fearful and anxious part, is on the side-
lines. She is worried about the pitfalls and hurdles on her journey,
but Bonnie's spirit is symbolized by the graceful, confident ice skater.
The message to Bonnie is that she should not worry; she, along with
her spirit, will "skate" through this ordeal without a hitch!

Her husband, who had been sitting there silently reading the
paper, jumped in, saying "by gosh, Bonnie, she's got it. That's exactly
what that dream meant!"

I was surprised by her husband's overwhelming enthusiasm for
something that most men probably would have dismissed as hen
clucking. But he was really quite animated. I'd like to think that he
actually did agree with my knee-jerk interpretation, although part
of me thinks perhaps it was more that he wanted to somehow be
upbeat and positive and this was his way of showing support. In
any case the results were the same. The three of us became terribly
excited by the prospects of this dream, and became very positive
about the outcome of her tests.

Had Bonnie been able to interpret that dream on her own, perhaps she would not have spent any time agonizing over the results of the test. And as a footnote to this incident, her test results were, in fact, negative. All that worrying for nothing! As of this writing, we have yet to uncover why cancer had resurfaced. We are, however, encouraged by the knowledge that her spirit is "skating" through this ordeal. Hopefully this little dream will be enough to quell her fear, help her find peace, and go on and live the second half of her life.

I see Bonnie now and then; she looks great. I always make a note to ask her about any additional dreams, but it seems as if they are no longer a concern. She is doing well now and in all likelihood has forgotten to pay any attention to other nocturnal messages. I, on the other hand, live for information from the dream state!

MRS. SANTA CLAUS

The more I volunteer the better I get at talking with the patients. I have learned to glean rather quickly those patients that are open and those that are not. Even if someone is talkative it does not necessarily mean that they are open. Many times talkative patients are uncomfortable with silence and use talk as a means of comforting themselves, quieting their innermost fears. By filling the air with empty chatter, they attempt to form a verbal smoke screen before their true feelings, their absolute anxiety. I can see it in their eyes. A little bit of small talk is fine, it's a good icebreaker, but generally, if the conversation is going to go deeper it usually happens rather quickly. Unsure of how often I will see these patients, I now, in addition to the dream question, try and weave a question or two into our conversations about their own thoughts on why they are sick. The results have been very interesting.

On one such occasion I was talking with an older woman, who reminded me of a good-looking Mrs. Santa Claus; full figured, full faced, full head of shimmery white hair. She was being treated for lymphoma. Initially, when we started talking she stated that she had been in a very traumatic car accident and felt that this was what brought on her cancer. Ever since that accident, she has been afraid to drive, afraid to leave her home. The accident occurred about four years ago. Then she stated that she had also lost her husband about the same time. She said that she missed him very much, that life wasn't the same without him. And then very abruptly, she looked me squarely in the eyes and said, "No, that's not true. I don't miss him at all. I hated the man! I hated being married to him. But in my day you just didn't get divorced. He had a nervous breakdown after my first daughter was born and never worked another day in his life. It was all on me to be the breadwinner and raise the children; he never lifted a finger to help me or to ever show his appreciation. To outsiders he was very helpful and friendly, but he never showed me the slightest consideration. I hated being married to him!"

By now she was crying and so was I. We were both crying over all those wasted years of pretense, crying over being someone she wasn't, with someone who didn't love her.

It was only after she started really talking and I started really listening; it was only after the routine remarks, the pat answers about being a widow and how much she missed her husband, that her deep resentment of all those lost years surfaced. Talking with me, a stranger, a hospital volunteer, gave her the opportunity to be authentic with her emotions. What did I know about her, her family, or her circumstances? It struck a chord with me. I too felt that way for a long time in my marriage. I felt that on some deep emotional level I wanted to stay home with my kids, but my obligation to earn money superceded every thing else. It was expected of me. It was part of the bargain. It was my idea of equality; it's what kept me independent, free. It's what fed my ego. It's what defined me, or so I thought.

I prescribed writing her dead husband a letter, an honest letter, telling him everything she told me and then some. "Keep the letter for a time, read and reread it, then when the time feels right, burn it, thereby releasing yourself from all those deep sources of pain and frustration."

In the meantime, I promised to be on the lookout for an older gentlemen to take her to a movie or dinner, which she said she'd love to do. I feel this woman has so much more living to do! Hopefully now she will begin to heal these wounds and go on with her life. The last time I saw her she looked great. Her hair was done; she was on her way to a party and had stopped off to get a treatment.

MY BROTHER'S KEEPER

It was also during this time that my Uncle Jack was diagnosed with lung cancer. He was a reformed smoker of 10 years who suffered from acute emphysema. I had several opportunities to visit with him and we would talk, play cards, and sometimes go out to eat. On one particular afternoon, Jack's wife mentioned something to me in passing that struck me as odd. She said that Jack didn't get sick until after he had returned from visiting his older brother Gene, who was dying of colon cancer that had metastasized to his lungs and brain. "Every time Jack would return from staying with Gene, his own condition would worsen," she said. Jack developed lung and rib cancer within weeks of witnessing his brother's deterioration.

In a subsequent conversation, my sister told me that my Aunt Stell had always noticed that whatever ailment Gene contracted, Jack would come down with something worse. For example, if Gene caught a cold, Jack would develop an upper respiratory infection. If Gene had a sore on his face, Jack would develop skin cancer in the same spot.

The next time I visited Jack, I touched on this subject briefly, asking him if there was any truth to his wife and Stell's speculations. Jack agreed wholeheartedly that there did seem to be a causal connection, but had no plausible explanation as to why. He responded by saying that it was "always that way."

Gene suffered serious bouts of mental illness and schizophrenia throughout his life. Some of Jack's earliest memories were of accompanying his brother Gene in the middle of the night. Although several years younger than Gene, Jack would take it upon himself to protect his older brother during his erratic, sometimes frightening episodes. Jack recalled walking miles at midnight alongside his catatonic brother. Many times Gene did not even recognize the brother who walked by his side.

Could such a strong bond between brothers exist? So strong, in fact, that one brother would assume the pain and suffering of another? If my Uncle Jack believed from a very young age that his purpose was to watch over his brother Gene, if, in his Mind, he was somehow responsible for Gene (and I think somewhere deep in the recesses of his psyche he did in fact believe this) then maybe his belief was so strong, that he willed himself unconsciously to the same or similar fate – cancer.

Jack dreams often. Of late he was dreaming of Stell and Gene, both now deceased. They are seated across a table from him. They are sharing a meal and talking to Jack, but Jack cannot understand what they are trying to tell him.

I sensed that Jack knew he was dying based on what we didn't talk about during my visits. There was one occasion, however, when he did voice some trepidation. I accompanied him to the oncologist's office. While waiting in the exam room, we talked about the word "forever" and how it is such a weird notion; forever heaven; forever hell. Either way, it upset him. I told him I remembered thinking similar thoughts. I labeled them "Eternity Issues." Jack was more concerned about forever "hell" and I announced, I guess rather defiantly, that I didn't believe in hell. What God would proclaim to be all loving, all caring, all forgiving and then create hell. Further I said, "How can you believe one and the other at the same time?" I told him I opted to believe in love and forgiveness – in my mind, the only lessons worth learning. Secretly I was hoping that Uncle Jack would start to wonder too about the nonexistence of hell other than in his own mind.

He was also worried about the body dying, ceasing to exist. I asked him, "Are you this body?" "Are you this hand, this leg, this lung?" He looked at me quizzically. I pressed, "Tell me what part of this mound of flesh is you. He could not answer. "Uncle Jack," I said "I know that your true essence, your true being will go on. This flesh will return to dust, as all of our bodies will; but the essence of who you are, Uncle Jack, will remain in our hearts; you will travel to where you go in your dreams, to where Gene and Stell wait for you." His slight, silent nod made me think that our conversation was of some comfort and hope to him.

Later that night, I started to think of the things I would remember Uncle Jack by: kindness and love, magic tricks, card playing, Brillcreamed black hair, a white 1962 Corvair that he let my younger sister drive, pennies raining from heaven every time he babysat us, Lucky Strike cigarettes in the chubby red glass ashtray next to his favorite green leather chair, his overly habitual love of the track, cracking our knuckles for quarters, his acceptance of every man, his wonderful sense of humor, his never-ending practical jokes, his ability to laugh at his own foibles, even in the face of death. It is my hope the Uncle Jack finds the way to healing before he leaves.

MORE PATIENT STORIES

I was surprised by the frequency with which common dream symbols surface in patients. Patients of different genders, with different diseases.

Since my early days at the Cancer Center I am now able to glean with more certainty the nature of the illness behind the patient. Some times it is merely through conversations with the patient or their loved ones that I am able to undercover areas in need attention. Sometimes this comes about through discussion of a patient's dreams. My own dream experiences have been extremely helpful in deciphering the language and symbols used in the dreams of many cancer patients, both men and women. For example vehicles and what the dreamer did for work are commonly used symbols in the dream state. But in addition to the, let's say, generic symbols there are often very specific symbols that only the dreamer will understand. In these cases, my own dream experiences assist me in knowing how to ask and what to ask the patient that will help uncover the message of their dreams.

KARSON

For some reason, I had missed a few days of volunteering so I went in on a Monday. There I met a guy named Karson. He had been recently diagnosed with lung cancer. Chemotherapy was administered first in an attempt to reduce the size of the tumor in his chest in order to operate. Karson looked to be about my age, mid-40s. He was a nice guy with an open manner, longish hair; I believe he told me he was an electrician. His wife and 3-year-old daughter were there with him. I was touched by the fact that his little girl wanted to sit in bed snuggled up against his side. He lay there in a semi-reclined position with one arm hooked to an IV and the other protectively hanging over his little girl's shoulder. Earlier I had overheard him complain to the nurse about his exhaustion and total lack of sleep as a result of the strange nightmares he was having. Of course my curiosity was peaked.

After introducing myself and getting Karson something to drink, I explained, as I do with all new patients, that I was treated for cancer eight years ago. This usually puts them at ease and provides an immediate bond. Karson had no trouble relaying two recurrent dreams to me. The first one was simply:

> *I am in a tower with a rifle but no ammo in the rifle. I am extremely frightened.*

I am surprised at how succinct this dreams presents his current situation. We wholeheartedly agreed that the tower in this dream symbolizes his isolation with cancer. He is alone, trying to fight it, but he doesn't know what to fight it with, symbolized by the lack of ammunition.

I can see that either he is a very trusting person or I have in short order earned his trust through the interpretation of this first dream. Before we embark on the second dream, I asked a rather impertinent question, especially in view of the fact that I had just met him and that I saw his wife there with him earlier. I asked if there had been any major emotional trauma in his life recently. I asked if someone had broken his heart, because the lungs and the heart are in the same chakra, one of the seven energy fields of the body.

Karson was quite surprised that I asked such a question. Not so much because it was so personal, but because it was so relevant. Shortly before his marriage, he had been involved in a tumultuous love affair for nearly 20 years. He had lived in Florida with an American Indian woman with a fierce temper. The relationship ended badly and he married rather quickly thereafter.

Now to his dream:

I am in my brand new 2000 Nissan pick-up truck, trying to run over a West Nile Crocodile in the muddy, swamp, but the huge tail of the crocodile keeps hitting the side of the truck. I know I must run over it, get over it, or kill it in order to pay off the debt on my truck.

To my way of thinking the truck symbolized Karson. It was how he viewed himself. He was a brand new pick up truck. However, I had no idea what a West Nile Crocodile represented. But Karson did. Over the years spent in Florida, he became an aficionado of these creatures, initially out of necessity. His old truck kept breaking down and as a result he would often ride his bike to and from work. It became vitally important that he understood the habits of these predators, especially when traveling home on a bike at dusk.

The nickname for the West Nile Crocodile is "man eater." By Karson's own admission, his former lover fit the bill. And so here was a very symbolic dream which basically said to "lift the debt," to release this burden you must "get over," "run over" the man-eater in your life. To heal yourself you must heal this relationship.

MARY

Mary was a very bubbly, vivacious, woman of Latin descent who was being treated for advanced-stage breast cancer. She had big brown eyes and a wide, bright smile that engulfed everyone at first sight. She planned her treatment day like a picnic. Usually family or friends accompanied her and they would spread out on her bed and play cards, eat a lunch they had prepared for the day and make the most of the time. We never really spoke much, since there were usually other people around and she seemed to be very hopeful, managing her way through this illness.

Months passed and for some reason unknown to me, her friends were now replaced by her husband. This was her husband by a second marriage. He was boyish looking, computer type who was clearly many years younger than she. He always brought a pile of papers, a brief case and other reading material with him. He would sit with Mary until she got hooked up and then would either submerge himself in paperwork or leave.

Mary eventually stopped responding to the chemotherapy. The light in her eyes was glazed over now. Her weight had dropped significantly and so had her smile. One day during her treatment, after her husband had left, I went over to keep her company for a few moments. Rarely did she dream, she told me, because she was taking a lot of medication. She could only remember one short dream. She dreamt she was trying to place a catheter in her husband's left leg. I was puzzled because I didn't understand what that was. She explained that she had been a nurse and that this is a medical procedure done "to open and clear a passage to the heart."

The dream was attempting to convey to Mary, in terms she understood, her need to find a way to make her husband love her. Her struggle was being married to someone that obviously didn't care for her. Unfortunately, the richness of this simple dream was wasted upon Mary because she had been trained only in the physical. Her strong medical background impeded her ability to see and understand the significance of this dream.

SARAH

Sarah teaches classes on Eastern religions at a nearby college and is being treated for colon cancer that metastasized to the lung. She is an articulate, attractive, well-kept woman in her early 50s. Her longish brown hair is gracefully giving way to gray. She stated that she seldom dreams because she is on several medications for anxiety and has difficulty sleeping. However, she probably doesn't need to dream often, based on the one and only dream she relayed to me. Initially she hesitated to tell me the dream. She asked if I thought she should seek the counsel of a therapist to help her interpret the dream. I told her that no one knew better than her what her dream was about; she just needed to take the time to talk it through, which is exactly what we did. She relayed this dream:

I am working at a gas station, pumping gas. The station

is located on a corner of two roads that intersect. On the one side of the main road is a high cliff and on the other side there's a sharp ravine. An older gentlemen, who appears to be inebriated, pulls into the station in a classic type car. I am pumping gas in his car and worried that he shouldn't be driving in his condition. In the meantime another car pulls into the station. This car is a BMW or some younger, trendier type of car, driven by an individual who is around 25 years old. There is another young person with the driver. The older gentlemen and the younger driver strike up a conversation and decide that they will race each other.

They pull out of the gas station and begin to drag race. The older driver losses control of his car, veers off the road and crashes against the side of the steep ravine. Immediately I try to call 911, but instead, in my confusion and haste, I dial 119. In a fairly detached, non-emotional way, I realize that the older gentlemen is now gone and it is pointless to call for help. I awake from the dream.

Within a few minutes, she was able to discern that the older gentlemen in the classic car represented her. The younger drivers represented all the students she teaches. In her own words she expressed her need to compete with the younger age group. She is intoxicated with "driving" herself to keep up with each new class of students. A part of her spirit fuels this need, represented by her "pumping fuel" into the classic car. The station is situated at an intersection, and, by her own admission, she realizes that she is now at a "crossroads" in terms of her health and life decisions. She feels that by letting the older gentlemen "die off" she is now ready to release her hold on youth. She is thinking about pursuing other interests besides teaching once she is out of treatment.

$\mathcal{M}$ARIE

Marie reminds me very much of my close friend Susan. She resembles her physically and also projects the same attitudes and personality traits. She's what you would call a real pistol. She is very genuine and interested in everyone. She is open to the other patients around her as well as the staff. She is always up.

Despite this loving, pleasant side of Marie I see that there is still fear and anxiety behind those big brown eyes of hers. We talk every week but only about the small things, not the big things. She has never really opened all the way. One day, though, she offered some insight through a dream she had. She wanted to talk about it because she didn't know what to think. She wanted my take on it. This was the dream:

I open an ancient box; thousands of black bugs of every description come rushing out, scattering everywhere.

Here was the first sign of Marie's other side. She was opening the part of her that she has kept contained – "boxed in" – for a very long time. Perhaps this represented her final release of fears and negative emotions, represented by the myriad of black bugs. She was anxious about the meaning of the dream. My thought was that since the bugs were running away from her then it was definitely a positive sign. It was a sign of cleansing. That which she used to "box" up inside of her; she has, of her own accord, now released.

WILLIAM

With each new encounter, I learn that every person is different and that different things affect people differently. Take William, for example. He was diagnosed with lung cancer. He was a large, pleasant faced man, ostensibly married to a devoted woman. His wife would always accompany him for his treatment and stay on top of all his appointments, procedures, etc. I didn't detect any hostility in their relationship; it was more like a mutual business arrangement. They were both attractive, well-kept people in their late 60s.

He seemed more fragile emotionally than her; she wore a mask of heavy makeup and had that frozen detached look. They were both retired and financially comfortable. I mistakenly thought that maybe the problem was a loveless marriage. It was only after spending a considerable amount of time talking with him over the course of many treatments that the underlying cause of his illness surfaced.

William loved the Boy Scouts. He volunteered many hours and went on countless camping trips over the years. Eventually he made his way into the Boy Scout hierarchy and then, for some inexplicable reason, he was overlooked for a certain position, eventually demoted, and then replaced altogether. He never recovered from being discarded from a group to which he was so devoted. He couldn't "get over" it.

Now to someone else this might seem almost laughable. But different things affect people differently and this man loved the Scouts. He loved everything about them and what they represented. The Scouts let him down; they broke his heart. In his mind, this was the ultimate betrayal.

+ + +

I once read that dreams are "unopened letters on your pillow." Opening these letters and deciphering their content can also prove extremely helpful in recovering from the physical effects of cancer, the surgery and chemotherapy. By paying attention to even the most far-fetched suggestions from the sleep state, tossing in a little bit of active imagination, the results can be downright surprising.

MARTIN

Martin was a tall, handsome, dark-skinned man with a slow, quiet smile and a soulful expression. He often told me how much he missed eating the foods he loved. He had to forego his fresh vegetables and heaping salads because the roughage played havoc on his lower intestines. He was receiving chemotherapy for colon cancer and was also recovering from surgery in that area.

He dreamt that he was pumping diesel fuel in his automobile. This simple dream easily depicted his predicament. The dream's message was that he was "fueling" his body with the wrong substance. He would ruin his car's (his body's) engine if he did not provide it with the proper "fuel." His car did not run on diesel anymore than his body operated on the junk food he was currently eating. The message was to return to that which he craved. So he gradually started to incorporate the salads and vegetables back into his diet. Hopefully, his intestinal tract adjusted.

ℰDWARD

Edward was a jovial grandfather-type with a shock of white hair. Since his diagnosis with lung cancer, Edward had been unable to eat anything. He could only tolerate liquids despite the fact that his doctor could find no physical explanation for his loss of appetite. It was blamed on the effects of chemotherapy, which is not uncommon. For nearly seven months he relied solely on milkshakes and high caloric liquid supplements until eventually he could no longer stomach even them.

Edward was more upset over his loss of appetite and weakened physical condition than he was over the fact that he had cancer. Routinely, I asked Edward if he was dreaming. The answer was always no. One morning we were talking and again I mentioned the idea of dreaming to help with his food dilemma. He said that that morning he woke up thinking about "Butterfingers." I mistakenly thought he meant butter on his fingers, but he countered, "No, no, Anne, I mean the candy bar "Butterfingers." I asked "Do you think you could eat a Butterfinger?" To which he replied, "Oh, I don't know. I doubt it; I'm not that crazy about them and you know I haven't eaten anything solid in so long."

On my way back from the cafeteria, I bought a dollar-size Butterfinger and ran into Edward's sister. "Here," I said half jokingly "give this to Edward." That evening he started nibbling the Butterfinger. It took him two hours to finish it. He then asked his wife to rush out and get another one before the store closed. Over the next few days he ate everything from potatoes to pot roast. His appetite has returned to normal and he is maintaining his weight. All it took was a small suggestion from the sleep state. "Butterfinger."

Dreams can also impart a sense of comfort when facing the unknown. These dreams are meant to soothe the soul during a difficult period, many times helping that person make the transition from this world.

$\mathcal{M}$R S . G

Mrs. G was wheeled into the outpatient area, wearing a hospital gown and curled up in the fetal position, clutching the bed rail with her hands. She was in discomfort due to fluid that had gathered in her abdomen. An older woman in her 80s, she must have been very attractive in her day. She cried softly, and then tried to hold back the tears. I couldn't tell whether they were tears of pain or fear or both.

She was dying. She had terminal ovarian cancer.

Later in the morning I was able to spend more time with her. We talked about her life, her children, and her husband. I asked if she dreamed and she said not really. Then she remembered a dream about her husband, who had passed on 30 years ago. In the recent dream, she saw him. She said he looked marvelous; very handsome, and that he was beckoning her to dance. She recalled how much they loved to dance when they were younger, how it was their favorite pastime, how it was actually how they met. I told her that she should be comforted by this dream. Perhaps her husband had chosen to appear now after all these years to let her know that he was waiting for her, just as she remembered him. I left her side momentarily and when I returned she seemed more pleased and peaceful; her doctor had also been by and removed the fluid from her abdomen. She was resting comfortably.

After one of my many blood runs to the lab I happened to turn the corner to outpatient oncology just as they were wheeling her out. She grabbed my hand, our eyes met. "Thank you." she said. Her words, her blue eyes, and the touch of her hand are still with me now. You see that was her gift to me.

I read a week later that she died.

✦ ✦ ✦

Dreams or experiences in the unconscious state can change one's life, can give their life new meaning and purpose.

*D*OTTIE

I mistakenly thought Dottie was a cancer patient when I came around to offer her lunch. She did not have cancer, but was in our treatment room receiving a blood transfusion. She was a pretty woman, petite with brilliant blue eyes and short blond hair. She was missing the lower half of her left leg, a result of whatever condition she had. We had a chance to talk for a while. She couldn't recall any dreams but she did tell me of a near-death experience she had.

Last year she became very ill. It started as a cold, developed into bronchitis and, unbeknownst to her, ended up as staphacoucus pneumonia. She was rushed to the emergency room, barely breathing. They were working on reviving her when she said she felt her self leave. She thought she was in an opium den where people were trying to give her opium; they kept saying it would make her feel better. She then fell into a dark hole and she was very fearful. At once, her daughter (who had been killed in a car accident) appeared encased in a tremendous span of white and gold gossamer wings. Her daughter scooped her up in her arms and told her that she had to go back, she wasn't to stay there. She said her daughter looked absolutely radiant. She said it was an absolutely unforgettable experience, like none she has ever had before or since. She felt total love and protection, total peace and exhilaration. As a direct result of this encounter, she firmly believes that her life's purpose is to raise her granddaughter, the only child of her deceased daughter. This woman is convinced that her daughter is with her at all times and is completely and utterly comforted by this experience.

ENERGY CENTERS
The Chakras

Patterns in patients are beginning to correspond with the Chakras, the seven energy centers of the body. Despite my limited knowledge of the chakras, I have been able to match the untold or discarded story of the patient with the corresponding chakra. It may take a while, but that important piece of information which in my mind accounts for their bout with cancer, that little detail buried somewhere deep in the chart, or their psyche, eventually comes to me, one way or another.

Two of the most common forms of cancer that we treat in women at St. Agnes are breast cancer and ovarian cancer.

The majority of women I have met being treated for breast cancer are simultaneously dealing with issues of the heart, which is the Fourth Chakra. They have either just lost their spouse, are about to lose a spouse through illness, or have lost a child, a brother or sister or someone very close to them. Or, they are women who are in the process of getting a divorce or otherwise involved in an unhappy love relationship. Initially, I was surprised how often these scenarios presented themselves. Now, it is so routinely evident that the heart has been severely injured in these patients, that it is the exception rather than the rule that I look to investigate further.

The common thread in ovarian patients was uncovered quite by accident. As I was filing charts one day, I would read a patient's name and realize that I knew the patient's husband as well, if not better than, the wife.

I went through every active chart and pulled each one in which the husband was as prominent in my mind as the wife. When I researched the type of cancer these women had, it was always ovarian. Rereading the chakra for that area of the body revealed that either controlling or being controlled is a prevailing issue. It was patently clear that these women were being controlled by their husbands. For example, if I asked how a patient was doing, instead of the patient responding in her own words, the husband would answer for her. The husband would go so far as to direct a wife where to sit in the treatment room, what to eat for lunch, when to schedule the next day and time of treatment. It was not uncommon for the husband to describe in detail the wife's chief physical complaint while she would sit there with a silent, stiff smile. One husband went so far as to direct when and where his wife would die. It was ultimately his decision. Don't get me wrong, I would say that for the most part these men loved their wives. They truly believed that this was a way of helping them cope with their illness. It was also their own way of coping through control. Furthermore, I am not suggesting that all women married to controlling men will get ovarian cancer. In many relationships, women lean towards the submissive role, and for their personality type a controlling husband would not be a problem. I believe it only presents itself as a problem when a woman denies her true Self and subordinates her role in the relationship over an extended period of time.

There were, however, two ovarian patients that didn't seem to fit this mold. In other words, I didn't know their husbands. These women had control issues of a different nature.

ℬ ARBARA

Barbara was an engaging, attractive, middle-aged, woman with a responsible position in the government. On her frequent visits for treatment, I would find her sitting quietly reading the Bible or writing in what appeared to be her journal. Later I learned that her book was actually a severely detailed, cryptic written reduction of everything that happened during the day. She recorded everything from the weather, to the people she came into contact with, her own vital signs, the treatment regimen, etc. This intense scribbling brought new meaning to the word "journaling." Her writing was so small that it was barely legible. She relied heavily on that black leather book. I am sure writing was her way of coping, perhaps it was her way of attempting to manage and control what was occurring in her life. I have no doubt that if she were to misplace that journal the personal repercussions would be devastating. This was her way of controlling herself.

ℒ OUISE

The other mysterious situation involved a wonderful woman named Louise. She was probably in her early 60s happily married to a man I seldom saw. We talked at length about her situation and I told her my observations of how I thought control played a role in ovarian cancer. Without hesitation she stated that for her entire life her mother had dominated her. She said, "My mother killed my brother, he died of colon cancer and as sure as I'm sitting here, she's going to kill me." She vowed to try her best to escape the clutches of her 80-year-old mother.

The few times I spoke with her husband, he concurred that his mother-in-law was most assuredly the source of Louise's unhappiness. In Louise's case, as much as she recognized the need to pry herself from the tentacles of her mother, ultimately she couldn't. Sometimes, the bond is too great to break.

JERRY

Jerry is an older woman with a raspy, deep-throaty voice. Dark hair, tall and thin, her looks and personality remind me of Rosalind Russell as Auntie Maime. She has been treated for lung cancer for the past three years. One day she sauntered over to me and we talked for a while. I briefly touched on the subject of dreams, which she told me she didn't have. She complained that she rarely slept, much less dreamed.

Then I saw her in the treatment room in a bed, not feeling too well. I walked by and she said "Anne, I was thinking about you the other night." I was surprised because we hardly knew each other. "Really?" I said. "How so?" Jerry told me that she was trying to get to sleep and that she was actually lying in bed saying to herself, "Jerry, you need to fall asleep. Jerry, you need to fall asleep." Then she heard another voice, which took her totally by surprise, saying *"Jerry, you need to wake up. Jerry, you need to wake up."* She said it was very bizarre. She thought perhaps she was dreaming. Then she thought that maybe she should cut back on her medication, but she realized that she hadn't taken any medication.

I understood what the semi-dream was trying to impart to Jerry. And I think somewhere deep in Jerry's mind she also had an inkling. But there was no crack in her window, she remained stalwart. She didn't want to discuss it any further. She didn't want to know what I thought. She didn't want to open her mind. She didn't want to "Wake Up."

MY THEORY

Every picture tells a story. Every patient tells a story. Behind every diagnosis of cancer there is a story to be told, there is a reason for their dis"ease." I believe that illness such as cancer is created in an unhappy mind. I believe that the mind moves matter. And that matter moves through the body and that the body becomes clogged with mutant matter that is the stuff of cancer. Mutating cells, cells gone awry.

There is not one person who enters the outpatient treatment room that was perfectly at peace and content with their life prior to getting sick. I am convinced that cancer is the end product of a mind manufacturing misthought. I believe that emotional traumas, betrayals, jealousy, envy, self-centeredness, control, fear, stress, depression, disappointments, despondency, religious extremists, tribal influence and a host of other scenarios cause cancer.

Cancer does not occur on a whim. The body does not drive itself. The mind drives the body just as sure as we drive our cars. Our body does not act independently from the mind any more than your car would take off at an intersection without you pressing the accelerator. The body is merely the "vehicle" in which the spirit navigates through this life. A person who is living an authentic life, who is, for the most part, truly at peace will not get cancer.

There are many more stories, many more thoughts on why people get sick, what triggers illness, and how patients heal. As one of the oncology nurses so aptly questioned, "Anne, how can you say this? We all have emotional baggage." She's absolutely correct. But I guess what I am suggesting is that its what we *do* with this baggage and also how we process these emotional traumas, disappointments, experiences, thought patterns, long held notions or beliefs. I suppose that this is what becoming conscious is all about. Learning to work with and through the experiences of our lives. Seek to see the lesson behind. Trust. Trust that our lives are on course, perhaps not the course we fashioned, but still on course. Trust that it is the right course.

AWARENESS

How can I explain the subtleness, the manner in which cancer makes your life different, how having cancer can, with a little bit of willingness from you, create more joy in your life?

Early one chilly Fall morning, after dropping the kids off at school, I found myself sitting behind a car at a red light in a busy intersection. The light turned green, but the car directly in front of me did not move. The light again turned red. I sat. My initial thoughts were, "Great.... I'm stuck behind this stupid young punk whose car has broken down." I could see that he was slumped down in his seat, his cap pulled all the way down over his ears. He hadn't made one single effort to move.

As I sat there waiting for the light to change, I noticed the song playing on my car radio. It was an old song from my hippie days by The Youngbloods, probably their only hit. I heard, "Come on people now, smile on your brother, everybody get together, try to love one another right now, right now, right now." And then I thought to myself, "Okay. Why is this particular song playing at this very moment and why do I happen to be the car positioned directly behind this disabled car?" I recognized that this was happening for a reason.

I decided to change my mind about the situation. I pulled up alongside of the car and showed my willingness to help. I was uncertain whether this guy would be friend or foe, and for a fleeting moment, I worried that perhaps he might even be armed. But I followed my hunch, I followed the song's directive.

As it turned out, the "punk" was an expectant young mother whose car had stalled as she returned home from dropping her husband off at work. She was very pregnant and didn't want to push the car in her condition. She was extremely grateful when I offered to help her. All it took to solve this problem was a call to her father-in-law on my cell phone.

Understand that I, too, was extremely grateful for this opportunity to be of some assistance to this young woman. I was grateful for the elation that I felt for the rest of that day and for many days afterward over this small, simple, synchronistic act of kindness.

Here is a perfect example of how a change in thought, a shift in perception, benefited me immensely. Had I acted in fear, I would have incorrectly assumed that this punk was not to be approached, that he was a stranger and a possible threat to me. Once the light changed, I would have impatiently swerved around the car and sped off. I might even have honked my horn as testimony to my total annoyance.

And yet hearing the words to this song changed my idea about the entire situation. I decided instead to act consciously out of love. To be open to helping someone else. To "smile on my brother." The wonderful feelings that accompanied this action are still a source of inspiration to me. It's all about living in awareness and using that level of awareness to broaden your experiences and enrich your life.

This is just one small example of how cancer can change your life. How, if perceived correctly, it can truly be called a gift. A gift of a new level of awareness, a new level of living.

My transformation of thought began with my experience with cancer. I am compelled to delve more and more into the spiritual side of illness because of the things that have happened to me.

These thoughts surface. Suppose for a moment that cancer should be welcomed. Suppose that dealing with this situation is the opportunity of your lifetime to become "aware," to become conscious, to actually see life in a new light. Cancer is your opportunity to become open and receptive, to learn about your connection to your own spirit, to another realm, and ultimately, to your Divine Source.

My experience with cancer jump-started my spiritual journey. It's unlikely that some other trauma or hardship would have produced the same results. Certainly, there were plenty of opportunities. Remember, the year or two preceding my diagnosis, bankruptcy was at my doorstep, exhaustion my constant companion. I was caring for four small children, working full time. My life was interspersed with midnight runs to the grocery store after spending hours rocking my son to sleep in the Children's Ward at Johns Hopkins. And I haven't even mentioned the laundry!

I'm not looking for sympathy, rewards or recognition. I have no doubt that my troubles paled in comparison to millions of others. My point is simply this – something had to shake my tree. Short of a nuclear reaction, nothing thus far had penetrated my programmed response of "I can handle this." Remember "I" could get through anything; nothing was going to break me. Despite all of these previous opportunities I had to surrender and become "aware," it never dawned on me to do so. I am definitely on of the denser ones, no question.

And what better than a life-threatening illness to propel me into my own spiritual awakening? I had to experience something that was so frightening and compelling. I had to face my own mortality.

I was a mannequin, poised, positioned, prepared to be tapped on the shoulder, to awaken. Something momentous had to occur to catapult me into the deepest recesses of myself. Something had to happen to show me that I was living my life unaware. Otherwise, how would I ever have changed? Why would I seek to learn about my higher self unless I came to realize there *was* a higher self.

I am reminded of a brief story about Jung. Evidently he had run into an old friend and Jung asked how his life was going. Jung's colleague responded, "Fine, just fine," to which Jung replied, "Oh, what a shame." Meaning that without our trials and tribulations we cannot possibly learn about who we are. I recently chuckled when I read a similar idea expressed on a sign outside a church, which read, "A good sailor is not made on a calm sea." And so the thrust of this book, this labyrinth of thought, is that cancer is the rough sea, the storm that awakened me.

The ENEMY *is* FEAR

"It is essential to remember that only the mind can create and that correction belongs at the thought level.... The very fact that you are afraid makes your mind vulnerable to miscreation."
A COURSE *in* MIRACLES

Once diagnosed, it is important to understand that cancer is not the enemy. Fear is the enemy. The catch phrase today is, "Fight the good fight, don't give up, don't succomb. Battle cancer. Be a cancer "survivor." Beat the odds; fight those cancer cells.

Yet when you take the attack approach to cancer, doesn't it by necessity involve "fear"? What if you were to change your idea about cancer? What if you were to welcome it as a challenge to your spirit and look forward to the lessons of love that cancer will teach you? Instead of fear, try serenity and peace.

Of course the mere suggestion of this way of thinking to someone who has just been diagnosed may seem preposterous, ludicrous, absurd, maybe even intellectually insulting. And yet its counterpart, fighting and fear, I believe, just increases the chances for the mind to continue its path of miscreation, thus making healing that much more elusive.

Healing, as described in *A Course in Miracles* is "essentially a release from fear."

> Only the mind is capable of error. The body can act wrongly when it is responding to misthought. The body does not create, and the belief that it can produces all physical symptoms.... The body is merely part of your experience in the physical world.
>
> It is essential to remember that only the mind can create and that correction belongs at the thought level... The very fact that you are afraid makes your mind vulnerable to miscreation.

Another emotion, anger, is certainly akin to fear. So is it fear that also creates the inability in people to express that anger, for whatever reason, fear of rejection, fear of reprisal, fear of hurting someone you love. Fear of facing the truth about your life and perhaps your most intimate relations. Bottling those emotions, however strong, and making the conscious choice over and over again to ignore these issues. Does this type of conditioning eventually miscreate at the cellular level?

Ar a recent cancer survivor celebration, one of the speakers approached the podium tickled pink, barely containing his brimming enthusiasm. Excitedly, he announced that within the next few months it was very likely that researchers would possess the ability to predict the type of cancer you would be prone to develop based upon your DNA structure! Hearing about this upcoming medical breakthrough had about the same effect on his listening audience as my cat dropping a dead bird at their feet!

Imagine how this was received. Now everyone connected to

cancer and actually all others as well can start worrying that much sooner about how and when their bodies may fail them. It stands to reason that these latest "advances" in detecting cancer genes may very possibly result in increased incidences of the very disease they are attempting to prevent. Talk about a self-fulfilling prophecy!

Do not underestimate the powerful influence of fear. If you begin to believe, as I do, that the mind does in fact miscreate, then the chances of an occurrence would also increase.

Work with me on this one. We already know that stress creates stomach problems, muscles tighten involuntarily, ulcers develop, etc. Why not go a step further and speculate that a stressful, fearful mind, in some people, creates cancer. Take lung cancer for example. Everyone believes that cigarettes cause cancer, that lung cancer is the result of smoking cigarettes, not of an ill mind. What if we looked behind the need to smoke? What if we studied the whole person, his or her thought patterns and beliefs? Would we find behind a compulsive chain smoker a nervous, fearful, unsettled persona? Someone that desperately needs, or so they think, to rely on outside stimuli to calm their nerves? Let me suggest to you that we look behind the fact that cigarettes cause cancer and seek to examine what kind of mind is at work. What kind of mind grabs for a morning drag before they even get out of bed? What kind of mind is convinced that they need these sticks to survive each day? What kind of mind will forgo many of life's true pleasures to suck down nicotine instead?

Furthermore, if cigarettes cause cancer then why do some people smoke their whole lives and never get sick, while others, who have never smoked a day in their life, get lung cancer?

The paradox might be solved if we look instead to the thought patterns, preconceived notions, general outlook and life attitudes

152 ◆ ANNE McNERNEY

of those that smoke and get sick. Where does stress factor into this equation?

I am an occasional social smoker. For example, when I get together with a bunch of girlfriends at the beach each summer, late in the afternoon we dig our feet in the cooling sand, watch the sunset with a glass of wine and sneak a cigarette for fun. I suppose we do this to feel like teenagers again – like we're really "breaking bad."

Isn't this entirely different from the person who reaches for a pack of cigarettes before reaching for the alarm clock every morning?

There are studies relating cancer and smoking which rely on laboratory rat experiments. Of course rats will develop lung cancer if they're stuck in a cage their whole life and forced to inhale cigarette smoke. How stressed out and unnatural is that? What animal wouldn't get sick, subjected to that kind of torture day in and day out? Are we any different? Is our rat race so dissimilar?

SURRENDER

Something else that needs to be addressed is the whole issue of surrender. True, more emphasis is now being placed on the patient's attitude and his or her general outlook. But I doubt if much is said in the hospital setting about surrender. Actually, the whole issue of surrender is completely misunderstood and totally underrated. If a patient can get past the fear, can release their terror, then the very next thing to do is surrender.

Why did I walk out of my house at dawn and turn my life over to God? No question, someone led me to do that. And I chose to go along with it, pink nightgown and all.

Surrender, in a spiritual sense, is the surrendering of your will, turning over your thoughts of control to God. This in no way means giving up, but rather giving over to a higher source in a deliberate, meaningful way.

Think about it. Your sense of control right now is an illusion anyway. You aren't in control of your life any more than you control the weather, nature, traffic on the beltway, the economy, the stock market, your neighbor, your neighbor's dog. The more I think about it the more ludicrous it is to think that beating ourselves up through strenuous workouts and exacting diets or doing , as I did, everything in a certain way will control our lives and our health. Believe me, there are plenty of people right now spending time in oncology wards who were in great shape, ate all the right things and thought they had their whole life mapped out, thought they could handle anything. I know, I was one of them!

There are also plenty of patients who, on the one hand, give lip service to "God's will," while on the other hand, desperately read every swinging piece of literature about the type of cancer they have, literally trying to manage their illness, counting white blood cells, buying unusual enemas, creating wild food concoctions, performing outrageous physcial regimens, trying everything they possibly can to stave off the inevitable. They attempt to postpone their moment in time when they truly surrender, when in fact they "let go" and "let God."

ACKNOWLEDGE *your* SPIRIT

"Corrective learning always begins with the awakening of the spirit, and the turning away from the belief in physical sight."

A COURSE *in* MIRACLES

Let's face it: today, doctors are considered demi-gods by the average layman. Millions of dollars and man-hours are spent each year on cancer research, so who are we to tell them anything! Patients, by and large, are guilty of placing entirely too much weight in what the doctors say.

Despite the fact that they get up each day like the rest of us, somehow we think they know more about us than we do! Too much stock is placed in their theories, their chemistry, and their statistics. Cancer patients must start taking more responsibility for their own healing, even if it means breaking out of their airtight Fort Knox mind vault and reading something a little different, becoming open to alternative ideas or exploring other avenues of healing.

Think of medicine as the mechanical parts of your machine or vehicle, your body. Then think of spirit, or lack thereof, as the part of your being that determines whether you stay healthy or become ill. Doctors are the mechanics that fix the broken parts of your vehicle. But this occurs once you've brought it in for repair. They look under hood and tell you what's wrong and how it can be fixed. What they don't ask and what you neglect to tell them is that your machine has been fueled by negative energy for years, or that this machine is carrying more baggage than one person ever should, or that this machine is never permitted to rest, never allowed to relax, calm down, be loved. It has been running uphill for a long time, or has been moving in a direction contrary to its wishes. And while the mechanic may fix the clog in the system, get it running again, it's really only a temporary fix unless the driver of this machine takes some time to go off road and personally uncover the areas of distress, discomfort or despair and correct his course.

You see the physician's / mechanic's passion is learning how the widgets and gadgets of your machine function. Their focus is to fix it. They are really not in a position to go out and tell you how to drive your car, how to live your life. That's your job, no one else's. That's your journey.

Hospital marketing hype claims to treat the whole patient. But I am not talking about doctors treating patients. I am talking about patients healing themselves and oncologists augmenting that healing. Here's where the subtle, or not so subtle, shift needs to occur. The shift in the burden of dis"ease," the shift in the patient's thought processes. The patient must begin the journey inward. Patients can no longer hand over the hefty trash bag of their life experiences to physicians and expect them to figure it out. "Here, doc, you do it. I don't know how to make my Self happy, I don't know how I got this way, I don't know where this stress, this anger, this depression, this anxiety , this sadness, this harmful view of my Self came from. You fix it, okay?"

Patients must reclaim the authority to heal themselves! Patients must begin to think that they played a role, albeit an unconscious and unintentional one, in the making of their current physical condition. ***Patients must come to realize that they are Spirit. They must acknowledge their Spirit.***

Patients must believe that they are the primary healers of their illness and that the medical staff is there to assist them in their healing efforts. A tremendous burden is placed on any oncology department to assume the weighty responsibility of permanently curing someone of cancer, essentially healing someone's life. Perhaps the thing to do is administer all available physical remedies in concert with treating the mind of the cancer patient.

Today doctors and other health professionals are becoming more inclined to include the patient's overall outlook as part of their file work-up. But I'm talking about more than just a cursory glance at a patient's disposition on a particular day. The focus should be on the patient's mind, not their molecules. Let's put the onus back on the patient to explain or at the very least, start to examine their life. Patients need to start developing their own ideas about why they are sick. They need to formulate their own thoughts on healing. What has or is happening in their life to explain this bout with cancer?

When we speak of holistic – rather, wholistic – medicine, it's not about encompassing all the different treatments and therapies, but instead relates to the Whole Person. Our treatment should "embody" the whole person, everything that influences or has been brought to bear on that person's life.

This is not to say that I am discounting all the various treatments available today. On the contrary, I am sure they have merit and are, in some cases, very effective. But perhaps their effectiveness is based on the notion that the mind believes in their effectiveness, thus resulting in some degree of efficacy.

Now is the time to think about the possibility that the mind can heal, that illness begins in the mind and it is there that we need to look for answers. Perhaps then the body will follow our lead, will take care of itself.

HEALING CENTER

While we're shifting the focus of healing we might want to examine the very place where healing would be most apt to occur.

I was struck by Uncle Jack's hospice care center. In many ways it fit my vision of what a treatment center would look like. It was a beautiful, moderate-sized building made of stone and wood that bore little resemblance to the sterile setting of a hospital.

A wonderful wisteria vine embraced a massive set of mahogany doors that opened to a lovely reception area. It was very quiet and peaceful, meditiative. There were large, softly colored rooms with plenty of comfortable oversized chairs and sofas. Wide windows and skylights bathed the entire area in light. This is the type of place where cancer patients should come first, not last! A place to relax, meditate, work with other cancer patients, read, reflect, dream, begin to uncover their source of disease."

In addition to these features, I would insist that the entire treatment area be above ground. Oftentimes, cancer centers are partially below grade and without natural light, presumably to accommodate the radiation facilities. It is essential to incorporate as much of nature as possible. Encase the treatment area in light. Preferably an atrium would be at the center, housing a very lush and beautiful garden of all types of plants and wildlife, if possbile. Fresh air would always be available. You would be able to hear the rain and feel the sun. A welcoming staff would be there to greet each new patient with open arms, with no egos or agendas other than to assist in healing. The staff would be comprised of former cancer patients, each with his or her own story of transformation and particular method of healing, available to assist any patient at a moment's notice. This is a place where others who have experienced cancer have the opportunity to give back, to offer their personal stories of how cancer was a gift in their life, helping others heal, giving others hope.

In addition, the physical areas would be arranged in fung shuei order, offering each patient views of the sun rising and setting. Massage therapy, therapeutic baths and saunas, meditational music, a library stocked with Spiritual and New Age reading materials would all be featured in this healing center.

Conventional medical treatments such as chemotherapy and radiation would be available, but such physical ministrations would not be the focus. A pivotal part of administering conventional therapies would be the agreement between doctor and patient to work in tandem, each handling their area of responsibility – the doctor: the physical; the patient: the spiritual. Then even if patients pass over, it isn't from despair; they are healed – and by healed, I mean they are happy. They have uncovered the source of their unhappiness. They have aligned their will with God's will. By their conscious decision to surrender, they in fact agree to trust in the Universe, in the Father. They are at peace with either outcome.

"Instead of relying on a few, wouldn't you rather open yourself up to the power of the Universe, trust in the Father and all living things

*to aid you in your journey? Or, put another way, would you want
to depend upon a few droplets, or the force of an entire ocean to
pull you through?"*

A COURSE *in* MIRACLES

REMISSION

I'd like to say a few words about words. Words from the lips of a doctor are extremely powerful. I cannot emphasize enough the power of suggestion and the power of the word. Take for instance the word *remission*. I recall one occasion while at St. Agnes when the spouse of a patient remarked to me how well I was doing, how wonderful it was to see me in *remission* for so many years. Initially, I politely murmured, "uh, yes." Then, in a nanosecond, I turned on a dime and stated rather emphatically that I was not in remission. I was "cured." She looked surprised and somewhat taken aback. I went on to say that my understanding of cancer cells is that they are created and destroyed daily and so I think it's logical that we include everyone in that "remission statement," and I mean everyone, including the entire medical staff. From my perspective, if you're cancer free, you're cured... until you're not. You see, I think doctors make a big mistake using words like "remission." It leaves the door open for that unwanted guest – fear. It's like placing an anvil over your head and waiting for it to drop. If there's no sign of cancer, that's a cure in my book.

Maybe statistics on "reoccurances" would favorably shift if (a) the patient fully participated in their healing, and (b) the doctor communicated that there are no statistics anymore, each person is an individual, that their fate is not housed as a number in a group of numbers, that the cure rate is as individual as the patient.

Keep in mind that a newly diagnosed patient is already feeling extremely unlucky. In their present fearful state, are we not sealing their fate by telling them that they've got a 40/60 shot of making it? Or that, on average, chemotherapy will extend their life by six months to a year.

The comment my radiation oncologist made still replays in my mind when Frank and I asked what he thought as we anxiously poured over my x-ray films under the light. "Anne, I'll tell you this: A patient came in here with a tumor the size of a pea and died. Another patient had multiple tumors throughout her body and she lived." In essence, what he was saying so succinctly and wonderfully was that he did not know why some people live and some people die; he did not want to venture a guess because that's what it would be: a guess. The odds are as unique as the patient.

Doctors might argue that making such a statement in essence gives a patient false hope. To the medical community, false hope means neglecting to tell the patient everything the doctor knows about their disease. Providing the patient with their professional assessment of what the statistics are for a cure, a remission, buying time, or palliative care. But there are problems with statistics. Statistics are numbers, not people. Behind every statistic, there is a number and behind every number sits a person who has a myriad of experiences, good and bad, who has preset ideas about themselves, about their life and what it's all about.

Let us take five such people who have the same cancer. Just

The GIFT *of* CANCER + 171

to keep it simple, let's say they are all the same sex, same age, and generally the same physically (i.e. – weight, height, blood pressure, etc.). And let's give them all the same treatement rgimen. Will they all pan out the same? No. Why? Because each one of them is unique. Each of them has different thoughts going on upstairs.

The first person was raised to believe that God punishes people who sin. This person dies. The second person suffers from low self-esteem and doesn't think they are worthy to live. This person dies. The third person realizes that their life is very precious now that it is threatened by illness and resolves to heal their unhappiness. This person lives. The fourth person just lost a loved one in an auto accident and sees no reason to go on. This person dies. The fifth person struggles with a toxic relationship, lives for a while, but, for whatever reason, cannot or will not change his or her circumstances. This person goes into remission, but eventually cancer returns and they die later.

So statistically speaking, this disease has a 20% cure rate. New treatment modalities may delay the physical process of the body responding to these misthoughts, but the reality is that unless patients heal their life, change their Minds, they will eventually fall prey to what the "experts" predict.

Let us begin by searching the mind as well as the molecules of a cancer patient. Let us agree that both doctor and patient participate equally in the healing process. One or the other does not dictate when life will end. That is left to the Divine. An oncologist may say "I have done all that I can." And that is where his responsibility ends and hope takes over. Because there is no such thing as false hope. Hope is hope. All hope is true, clear invincible belief in the power of the Mind and the will of the Divine. Hope comes from the ability to trust in the outcome whatever that may be. Trust that by aligning your thoughts, actions and will with that of the Universe that everything is as it should be. By interfering in Divine Will, you are working against the Universe and all it has to offer you. This does not mean giving up. This means recognizing that there is a much greater Force at work, and that you should align your Self with that Force. By doing so all that needs to happen will happen in its own time and space. All that is needed is your awareness and willingness to be guided.

And if you have done your work, if you have done your part, then you will know truly what His plan is for you. And it will be all right. You will be happy. You will be healed.

IGNORANCE *or* INNOCENCE

Is it pure ignorance or innocence on my part? Do I regard this whole area too simplistically? Do I think that if you find the source of a person's fear or unhappiness this gives that person a better chance of healing? Why do I feel so compelled to write this book? Why do I feel I can help cancer patients ovecome the obstacles to their happiness? What makes me think I can pull them through?

I suppose I have more questions than answers. But I guess if I waited to receive all the answers I would never finish this book. Another thought. Is an ounce of prevention really worth a pound of cure in terms of cancer? I'm not sure. Should we really put that much effort on the prevention of cancer? Suppose cancer does occur for a reason. Should we really try and thwart the growth that can come from this disease? If this seemingly traumatic event in my life had been detoured by a new scan, a DNA test or some drug, I would probably still be running around like a headless chicken. If someone offered to reverse the last eight years of my life, I would have to decline. I am much more content with the way my life is unfolding now. There is a greater sense of peace, of order, of purpose. I couldn't return to the old way – not knowing why I was alive, for what reason.

And what of the dream that turned my life around? What of

the strange message that made me venture back into the unknown, into the land of a thousand questions?

"Don't you think you should be doing research on *lymphoma*? After all, you were *a million to one*, your cancer was *perfect*, the *best*, of the *highest order.*"

Is it by writing this book, by volunteering in oncology, by reconnecting to a part of my life I mistakenly thought I should leave behind? Is it by working together with other cancer patients, I am returning, researching for answers to very big questions, not just for me, but for all others that find themselves in the very place I was so many years ago?

Would today's pathology report reveal that I did have *lymphoma*, not breast cancer? Or, was the word *lymphoma* used because that's where the cancer was found, in the lymph nodes? Or, does all cancer begin in the lymph nodes?

One in a million could have been referring to the type of cancer I had. According to my doctors, it was very rare, perhaps so rare that only *a million to one* contract it. Or, was my experience with this disease a model for others, a template of sorts?

In hindsight, I can now say that the cancer I had was *perfect*. It did change my life forever; it made me real. it was the *best*, and probably the only way for me to become conscious. It was from the *highest order*. My cancer was from a much higher level, a much higher form.

My dreams, the symbolic songs, the calm, the knowing, the quiet peace. I marvel at the mystery of it all. Fear has been replaced with a sense of wonder and excitement. I cannot be sad for people who have cancer. I can only hope that some day they will realize, as I did, that this could be the best thing that ever happened to them, if they let it. And that it has happened for a reason. And that once you uncover the reason, you will begin your journey home, you will begin to heal your life and you will begin to enjoy a life truly lived.

Now I have a passion. Yes, now I know my reason for being. Had I not followed the advice offered by someone, a spiritual guide perhaps, when I awoke from that fateful Saturday nap, had I not reached deep under my arm, I can say without a doubt, I would not be here today; I would never have discovered the lump. Surely, I would not be writing to you if I had relied solely on my annual mammograms and occasional health checkup.

There is a reason I am here. There is a Divine Plan for all of us. This much I know. And it continues to unravel even as I sit here and write in between loads of laundry.

Coming down the home stretch of this book, the following dream occurred:

I am standing in a line, a long line, many ahead of me, many follow me. It appears as if I am midway up the line. The line is moving slowly uphill. I get the impression that this line eventually leads to a gate, or a garden of some huge edifice. In any event, I feel my turn is now approaching. I mention to the person standing behind me that I need to get out of line for a moment to parallel park my car between two other cars. A black car and a white car. I feel anxious and worried. I see this oppor-tunity to park my car, but I don't want to lose my place in line and I don't want anyone to get angry with me when I return to my place in line. The person behind me, always unknown to me, pats my right shoulder reassuringly and lets me know that it's okay. It's okay for me to park my car there. My place in line will be held. It will be all right.

My take on this dream is that I am on my path, my journey. I am not alone; many others are on theirs as well. The line, or path, leads to the same place for each of us. The time is coming when I will enter into my true being, into the garden of my life. I have been waiting for my turn, for the opportunity to make my contribution, to make "my move" between the black and the white. That to write this book means stepping "out of line." I am afraid that what I am saying will ruffle feathers and that once I step out of line by saying the things I have said here that I will not be allowed back in line, that I will lose my place. And yet, as in other dreams, the mysterious someone behind me acknowledges my feelings and still urges me to go forward assuring me that it will be all right.

Despite the fact that my dreams are much more infrequent now, I am encouraged by this dream that I am on the right path. I also interpret less nocturnal guidance, to mean "Yes, Anne, you have caught my drift. Finally, you are beginning to do what you were meant to do."

The G I F T

Cancer is just the beginning. It is the portal to your new level of awareness. Seek to use this opportunity to understand and heal the part of your life that continues to make you unhappy. All that is needed is to discover the source of your unhappiness.

Examine your life. There is someting there that has to be changed. Those of you that are undergoing this ordeal, transform. Use this opportunity to uncover your real Self and the real purpose of your life.

Start believing that everything, and I mean everything, happens for a reason. Even this, right now the most awful, most tragic, most devastating, most painful, most trying time in your life.

Work with it. Become detached from the fear. Look for love; act as love. Become the wonderful person you are. Recognize life's most precious gifts.

Go inward. Don't be afraid. This is not the end. You are just awakening now. You have stopped sleepwalking. You are finally becoming aware, conscious, you are joining others as they too search for the truth and beauty.

Work at releasing all judgements. You and I are not in a position to judge others. Recognize that what you see is illusion, that it is what you feel that is truth. If you feel negative thoughts, go inward, that's where the problems lie. Change your Self. Change your perspective.

Don't hold grudges. I know this is hard. I never said it was easy. Grudges are the worst. They build in you like a cesspool. Harboring and wishing ill on others will only bring pain to you. If you believe that you and I are alike, are really of the same stuff, and if you love yourself, then it stands to reason that you love everyone. So don't hurt yourself by hurting others.

Forgive yourself for all the unloving things you did in your life. Remember you were sleepwalking then. You didn't know the truth. You were unaware. You are better now; you are awakening. You are on the verge of a new level of understanding.

Have compassion for those that have not yet awakened, for what they are missing right now – for not experiencing peace as of yet, for still running around looking for what is important in their life, for trying to fill the void.

Dream. My hope is that through my story you will begin to see the potential dreams can have in your own life. We all dream. Those that claim they don't must be patient, must be open to receiving them. By focusing at night, instructing oneself to "remember that dream." Then, upon waking, work with them; ask yourself questions about the dream, what each person, place or thing represents. The fact that you are dreaming is a very hopeful sign. They are pieces of your psychic puzzle, brought to you to help you heal your life, to help you become whole. Your dream sense is a very real sense, and once developed, it is as real as the other five, the ones you can touch, smell, hear, see and taste. It is a knowing that is as absolute as these.

Remember Olsen's dream, the directive to "get over" the man-eater in his life. Remember Bonne's dream, that she will "skate" through these obstacles. The mere fact that these dreams occurred serves as a clear example of divine providence, intervention, or whatever you want to call it. Here were specific messages, sent from whom it does not matter. The point is that a force beyond their control, outside their realm, was attempting to guide or instill a sense of peace, a powerful intention that "all is well."

Where do these dreams come from? I don't have the answer. But the fact that they happen at all is the real mystery. Accept the mystery; work with it; let it guide you, comfort you, inspire you, and compel you to live your life consciously. Isn't it odd that conscious living sometimes means relying on the unconscious, the subconscious, the mysterious? It means letting go of your notion about what is real and what is not. It means working with the Universe – all of it. What is both seen and unseen, understood and unknown.

Use your innate abilities to heal your life. Cancer is just the hook that grabs you around the neck and drags you off life's vaudeville stage. Once healed you realize how much you'll never miss dancing and singing and performing badly to an audience of others' expectations of who you are and what you should be doing.

Cancer is your ticket to your real life. Cancer is your passport to the life you were truly meant to live. Wouldn't you rather live your life authentically than live an entire lifetime of a "what I'm supposed to do" life.

Surrender. Picture yourself tubing down a river. You grab onto a low-lying branch and end up in a small, whirling, side pool. You spin around over and over, repeating the same cycle over and over again. You've stalled your development; you're hanging on to what you think is important; you're hanging on to control. And yet you are in such a small little sphere that, if you fail to release, eventually, the water will build up around you and drown you, overcome you. So let go of that low-lying limb; give up control; relax in that tube and feel the exhiliration, the speed, the powerful force of the river of life swirling you on to your destiny!

Instead of doing, try being. That's much more important. The doing will follow the being. Try being "in service" to others. The rewards are tremendous. If you have had cancer, make sure that you are now doing what you really *feel* you should be doing. Change your life now. Go ahead – you have a wonderful excuse! You had cancer! You are now entitled to start living authentically. It's part of your healing process. So go ahead and change. Change whatever it is you feel must be changed now that you realize that your life is not a dress rehearsal.

Don't think for one minute that I have mastered any of what I have said here! It is not an easy task, unlearning and undoing takes time. So be patient with yourself; love yourself; forgive yourself. Stay open to the positive energy that you emit and attract.

LEAVING *the* NEST

Leaving the hospital nest is sometimes as frightening as entering for the very first treatment. For many patients, ending therapy is a very stressful time. As patients count down the number of treatments, they also realize that the tight tether to their doctors and support staff is loosening. Soon, they will return to the rest of society, they will be "out there." As much as they want their chemotherapy and radiation to end, they don't want the safety net of doctor visits, nurse assessments and lab draws to dwindle. While in the protective range of monthly visits, they enjoy the sense of security that medical monitoring of their body brings.

This is because patients have not yet become aware of who they are. They are trying, albeit unsuccessfully, to put their life back the way it was before they were diagnosed. They are trying to return to "situation normal." But their lives will never be normal again. Nor should they want them to be! Their lives should take on a new level of living, a new level of joy. The joy of being alive. The joy of loving. These patients have not yet made the connection to something greater than themselves and their bodies. That is why it is so important to start the spiritual journey, to become open to their higher self, to realize that cancer is not the enemy, that the body did not betray them, that the body merely responded to their negative, despondent thoughts.

Once you understand that you are more than body, that you are Mind and Spirit housed in a body, then you can begin the thought processes to heal yourself, your Whole Self. By using your experience with cancer to become more aware of your higher Self, your greater good, your purpose and ultimate contribution here, you will expereience joy. And when you experience joy, you will love what cancer has done for you. And when you love what cancer has done for you, then you can no longer fear that which you love. This is the gift of cancer.

THE END?

The toughest part of writing this book is the ending. Because, quite frankly, I don't have an ending. Is there really one? My journey continues, as does yours. The question is, will what I have written here make a difference in someone's life, in the life of a cancer patient? I hope so.

On a side note, I will miss sitting here at my computer, listening to the familiar rhythms of the rinse cycle of my laundry.

Perhaps it is fitting to end with a dream.

A few weeks ago I awoke with an image in my mind. No action, no words, no thoughts, no songs. Just a simple picture of a healthy green plant in a pot. A house plant. The roots of this plant were breaking through rich dark soil, protruding thick white roots surfacing, knuckling up against the sides of the pot.

The dream was depicting a plant that had outgrown its container. It had become root bound. And so the dream depicts the need to expand, to spread out, to move beyond the container I find myself in. The plant in this dream is significant. It was an aloe plant, the plant of healing.

As I said earlier, now I have a passion. I love talking and working with cancer patients. I can see the benefit in bringing hope to them, in helping them uncover sources of dis"ease" in their life. Those who have touched me and whom I have touched will be part of my experience forever. With each encounter, there are new eyes with which to connect, and new truths to discover. There is hope. There is hope of healing, whether one lives or passes over. There is hope that this gift of cancer will heal our lives.

FURTHER READING

During the course of the past three years, books have come to me sychronistically, as perhaps this book is coming to you. Much of what I have said here has been birthed from the richness of reading *A Course in Miracles*; *Seat of the Soul*; *Conversations with God*; *There are no Accidents*; *Awakening in Midlife*; *Memories, Dreams and Reflections*; *Anatomy of the Spirit*, *Why People Don't Heal and How They Can*; and *Love, Medicine & Miracles*.

I have been reading many other books as well, but these come to the forefront of my mind and are the ones I recommend to others most often.

Your path will be your own. And once on your journey, stay open to suggestions you receive from friends, family, even the guy on the bus and the waitress in the restaurant!

"Write the book; the research will follow." Every patient tells a story. I want to hear your story, your thoughts, your comments, your dreams. Reach me at anne@resonantgroup.com, or at the book's accompanying web site: www.giftofcancer.com.

ACKNOWLEDGMENTS

There are many people that come to mind when I think about acknowledging those that have helped me bring this book together.

There's my dear friend, Linda Gentry, for her kitchen-table wisdom, great java and homemade coffee cake on the many mornings we would talk after dropping the kids off at school. Then there's also my informal mentor and confidant, Sister Theresa Mary, who, with her quiet and thoughtful ways, has inspired me to do more and who unwittingly brought Kevin Atticks and Resonant Publishing, my publisher, and I together. Kevin's friendship, guidance, and expertise in selecting my editor, Gemma Bridges, and my designer, Kate Ryan, has been invaluable.

I am forever grateful for my rekindled best friendship with Debbie Skipper, for without our Sunday morning telephone soirées I would have never known that she, too, walks with me on this journey. And, of course, my great friend Susan Bowden, for her fierce passion about all of life and her unfailing support and encouragement of this book.

Special thanks to Ed and Em, Denise, Dennis, Laura, Jimmy, Mary and Joanne for their quiet strength and support, and their unconditional acceptance of me, as difficult as it is at times.

And to the many staff members and patients at St. Agnes

Hospital, especially the unsung heros, Al, Amy and Lewis, who give
and receive love every day in the name of hope and healing.

Printed in the United States
29278LVS00002B/13